C000085772

EAST CHESHIRE WALKS
~ from Peak to Plain ~

Graham Beech

Publishing history: first edition 1985, reprinted 1986, 1987; second edition 1988, reprinted 1989, 1990, 1991, 1992, 1994; third edition 1996, reprinted 2000; fourth edition 2005; reprinted 2007.

Published by Sigma Leisure – an imprint of
Sigma Press, Stobart House, Pontyclerc, Penybanc Road, Ammanford, Carmarthenshire SA18 3HP

British Library Cataloguing in Publication Data
A CIP record for this book is available from the British Library.

ISBN: 978-1-85058-884-9

Typesetting and Design by: Sigma Press, Ammanford, Carms

Cover photograph: Cumberland Clough by Graham Beech

Maps: Bute Cartographics

Text photographs: © Graham Beech except where stated

Printed by: Berforts Group Ltd

Preface

In 1985, I began the first edition of this book with the following words:

"This book first came about as a result of my own walks in the Cheshire countryside. Although I have been interested in country walks for longer than I care to remember, it was only when I moved north to this area in 1980 and, a year later, joined the Ramblers' Association, that I really began to enjoy walking as a hobby. Another benefit was that I learned more about the east Cheshire area in three months than I had in the previous twelve."

Since I wrote that first paragraph over twenty five years ago, the book has undergone several changes, resulting in a series of revised editions in which essential changes were made and a few new walks added. In the third edition, a 20-mile challenge route was also included.

The fourth edition, however, was a major update. Each of the original routes had been rewalked and the directions revised to reflect changes 'on the ground' – anything from new or missing stiles to diversions due to roads, housing developments or, most significantly, the second runway at Manchester Airport.

Some things, however, have not changed: my enthusiasm for country walking, the delights of the counryside on my doorstep and the pleasure of inspiring others to get out there and enjoy it for themselves. The walks are fundamentally unchanged: they continue to reflect the varied terrain of East Cheshire – from the plains of Mobberley through the hills surrounding Bollington to the windswept moorland on the Cheshire/Derbyshire border. There really is something for everybody here!

As indicated earlier, my inspiration for this book came from the many happy days spent in the countryside with members of the East Cheshire Group of the Ramblers Association – now approaching a membership of 1000. We sometimes wonder what the vast majority of our members get up to during the weekends, but the 'hard men' (and women!) still enjoy each other's company after two decades – soaking up the summer sun and facing up to most of winter's challenges. Several members – includng Mike Harding, John Edwards, Joyce Blanchard and, of course, my wife Diana – have been good companions (and helpful critics!) while checking some of the walks.

I'm not planning any further major changes, but I said that after the last revision! So do write in and tell me if you encounter any problems and, of course, if you enjoy the walks. Who knows? I might even catch sight of you, book in hand, with a puzzled frown as you try to decide what on Earth some instruction means. So if I step up to you while you're out for a walk, please believe me when I say "I wrote that book".

Graham Beech

Contents

N

Styal
Poynton
Wilmslow
A523
Mobberley
Adlington
A538
Bollin
Valley
Pott
Shrigley
Lyme
Park
Kettleshulme
Knutsford
Alderley
Edge
Bollington
Prestbury
A537
Goyt
Valley
Capesthorne
Macclesfield
Tegg's Nose
Siddington
Macclesfield
Forest
Gawsworth
Sutton
A34
Wildboarclough
North
Rode
Wincle
Congleton

0   1mile

INTRODUCTION

You won't see signs saying "Welcome to East Cheshire", but I take it as that part of Cheshire extending roughly from Mobberley in the west to The Tors ridge above the Goyt Valley in the east – giving a fairly even split between the peaks and plains. Macclesfield is in the centre, but access is easy from Manchester, Stockport, Congleton, Knutsford and many other northern conurbations.

There have, of course, been some changes over the past two decades. New roads have been built and traffic volumes have increased significantly. Out-of-town shopping centres have appeared, and towns and villages have had to adapt to survive with more bars and building societies and fewer 'useful' shops. Many village shops that were handy for walkers have closed, together with several cafés and even a few pubs.

But the landscape itself has not changed greatly. In lowland Cheshire, smaller fields have been combined with the occasional loss of a field boundary – for nowadays only large farms can prosper. And I do mean large: one farmer I met told me that he over-winters 4000 sheep, a far cry from the days when a living could be made from a few acres. Likewise, some remote farmsteads and barns have been abandoned, and others have been replaced by 'executive-style' houses or adapted as gentrified dwellings, often with a change of name. At a more detailed level, many stone walls have crumbled, some stone stiles have completely disappeared and others have been replaced with gates – these being welcome as they provide better access to the countryside for the less nimble.

Apart from numerous farm and barn conversions, the hill country in East Cheshire has remained remarkably free of intrusive new buildings – and for this we should be grateful both to the Peak District National Park and the Campaign to Protect Rural England (CPRE). We have been spared the curse of the windfarm, tempting though it must be to site such eyesores on the hills of the Peak District. Arresting or reversing global warming is desirable but is wind power the answer? Politicians have targets to meet, manufacturers have turbines to sell, and farmers and landowners have been quick to see an additional income source. But 1000 turbines can only generate (according to CPRE data) 0.25% of the total UK energy requirement – and then only when the wind blows.

Renewables have their place, but nuclear power stations don't produce greenhouse gases. End of rant – tell me your views!

How to use this book

In addition to the 20-mile 'challenge' route at the end of the book, there are nine main sections which deal with the following areas in alphabetical order:

Adlington, Poynton and Disley

Alderley Edge

Bollington

Gawsworth, Wincle and Congleton

Kettleshulme and Rainow

Prestbury

Siddington and The Peovers

Wildboarclough

Wilmslow and surrounding area

Each section has some background information and each walk starts with an 'at a glance' section, arranged in a standard format. The main points to remember when choosing a walk are:

🐾 The 'duration' is the time it took me to complete the walk. For longer walks, when darkness is likely to be a problem, start early so that you are sure to get back in time. Allow extra time if leading a group or walking with children.

🐾 The starting point is given both as a description and as a grid reference, e.g. SJ849713. For an explanation, see the section on Maps on the next page.

🐾 The walks are graded:

Easy: mostly flat with few obstacles.

Moderate: some hill climbing and/or rougher terrain.

Strenuous: best avoided if accompanied by a young family! (I've yet to find a really strenuous walk in East Cheshire – it's gentle, rolling country with hill walks just tough enough to work up a thirst.)

The walk descriptions are believed to be correct at the time of writing, but it is likely that signs, stiles, trees and other landmarks may disappear and new ones appear in their place. I offer my apologies to any landowner whom I may have slighted in describing difficult access to a path – the problem could well be resolved by now.

What do you need?

Apart from this book and an OS map – very little. Disregard those who want to load you up like a Victorian explorer – you're going to enjoy yourself. Here's what I regard as a sensible minimum:

- **Waterproofs** – the types that 'breathe' are best. Rainfall in Cheshire is statistically no worse than anywhere else, but it sometimes seems as though it is.
- **Boots** – I wear boots most of the time, though I've switched to lightweight walking shoes for the summer – why carry excess baggage on your feet?
- **Rucksack** – the smaller the better, within reason. Pack sufficient food and (more important) drink – better too much than too little.
- **Compass** – when used in conjunction with an OS map, this takes the guesswork out of walking. Be sure to get the type with a flat Perspex base (e.g. the 'Silva' range) and practise in the garden before using it for real.
- **Map** – and learn how to read it. OS maps are so accurate that a GPS is unnecessary in the UK, but fun for those who like gadgets.
- **First Aid Kit** – you must be able to cope with life's little emergencies!

To this list you can add walking poles (if infirm – otherwise, they're fashion accessories for walks in East Cheshire), whistles and what-have-you. I prefer to keep life simple.

Maps

Each walk contains a sketch map and detailed directions, which should be sufficient to enable you to navigate your way successfully from start to finish. They are only *indications* of the routes and are definitely not replacements for OS maps. Also – and **very important** – the maps are drawn to fit on the page without rotating the book. This means that **'North' is not necessarily 'up'**. I strongly recommend that you invest in one or more of the 1:25,000 scale maps for the area covered by this book: Explorer 268 (Wilmslow, Macclesfield & Congleton) and Explorer OL24 (The Peak District – White Peak Area).

In addition to the usual topographical symbols (for churches and the like), the most useful map features to follow are field boundaries. This is because they are obvious linear landmarks, so even if you do veer off-course, you can follow the line of a hedge or wall to where you ought to be. Many hedges have been removed in the name of progress, but the ones that remain are invaluable because you can so easily relate the field that you are standing in to its outline on the map. Note: field boundaries are shown (as black lines) only on the larger scale 1:25,000 OS maps.

Grid references in this book (mainly for starting points) comply with the OS convention and, as such, they pinpoint any location. For anybody unfamiliar with the notation, here is how it works, using OS Explorer 268 (Wilmslow, Macclesfield & Congleton) and map reference SJ843786:

(i) The first two letters (SJ) identify the relevant part of the national OS mapping system. The country is divided into grid squares from 'NA' in the north-westerly tip of Scotland to 'TV' off the end of the south-east coast. Our area is within the 'SJ' and 'SK' squares – there is a handy diagram on OS maps to identify the relevant square.

(ii) The first three digits are called the eastings. Look at the horizontal numbering on the Explorer map until you find, in the example above, 84. Then count off three of the ten imaginary smaller divisions between 84 and 85 – this gives you your east/west position.

(iii) The last three digits are the northings. Find the vertical numbers 78 and 79 on your map and count off six of the ten imaginary smaller divisions between them. This is the north/south position.

All you now have to do is find the intersection of the two positions. You should find that it's at Alderley Edge railway station.

Public Rights of Way – and other countryside matters

The footpaths in this book are all believed to be on public rights of way or permissive paths unless otherwise noted. A number are unsigned, either accidentally or deliberately, but they are still rights of way. Since 2005, several areas of 'access land' have been created under the Countryside and Rights of Way Act – for example, in Lyme Park and around Wildboarclough – giving new rights of access to open country. Mindful of these developments, the Countryside Agency introduced a code which suggests:

🚶 Be safe – plan ahead and follow any signs

🚶 Leave gates and property as you find them

🚶 Protect plants and animals, and take your litter home

🚶 Keep dogs under close control

🚶 Consider other people

Expanded information can be found by searching the official website: www.naturalengland.org.uk. I devised a similar set of guidance points a few years ago after correspondence with the National Farmers Union, and they seem just as valid today:

Walkers

Keep to the definitive Rights of Way (except in Open Access areas) as shown on current OS maps.

Only use diversions when officially signposted.

Where a path crosses cultivated farmland, walk no more than two abreast to avoid unnecessary damage.

Use stiles where provided. Do not damage walls, fences or gates.

Keep dogs on leads whenever a right of way crosses farmland.

Leave gates as you find them (close them if it is clear that they ought to be shut).

Avoid injury by keeping away from animals and machinery.

Farmers

Know your paths and waymark them. If paths need to be ploughed, reinstate them.

Do not confuse walkers with concessionary paths. Apply for proper diversions.

Ensure that paths are not obstructed.

Provide stiles and keep them in good order.

Know your rights under the Dogs (Protection of Livestock) Act, 1953.

Provide stiles or, at least, easy-to-use latches.

Refer to HSE guidance for cattle on rights of way.

When paths cross fields you may have a problem – if only just a struggle with your conscience: should you cross the field, possibly walking over a crop, or go around the edge, adding time and distance? Legally, if a public right of way exists you are within your rights to follow it unless an official diversion has been granted. Why put up with a half-mile detour when the right of way is a straight line? If no diversion exists, a farmer must leave the footpath intact and

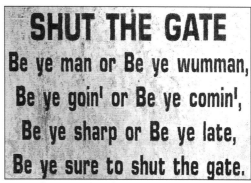

SHUT THE GATE

Be ye man or Be ye wumman,

Be ye goin' or Be ye comin',

Be ye sharp or Be ye late,

Be ye sure to shut the gate.

Sign seen near to Saltersley Hall Farm

uncultivated but in practice, the legal line of a path is often lost in this way. Where the routes in this book do cross cultivated fields it is because, at the time of writing, such diversions have either not been applied for or have been rejected. I do, however, have some sympathy for the NFU's proposal for temporary (seasonal) diversions.

Quite apart from the above, modern farming practice dictates that small fields are merged for ease of manoeuvring machinery – but with a loss of hedgerows and a subsequent reduction in habitat diversity. So far as walkers are concerned, footpaths that used to follow field boundaries may run higgledy-piggledy across new 'superfields'.

It makes good sense to leave paths as they are shown on OS maps – but I feel that walkers should be pragmatic when they encounter very minor diversions that really are of no inconvenience. If you encounter a persistent problem with a path, first and foremost be sure of your facts. Discuss it with the landowner or, to take it further, refer to the helpful website for the rights of way unit: http://tinyurl.com/2udag6r (the actual URL is so long that I've used the excellent TinyURL rather than risk a typo!).Or contact: Public Rights of Way Office, Phoenix House, Clough Road, Winsford, Cheshire CW7 4BD (Tel: 01606 271830)

A Load of Bull?

The grazing of bulls on land crossed by public paths is a persistent problem. Occasionally, a farmer may graze a bull deliberately to deter walkers or try to intimidate with a 'beware of the bull' sign. In such cases, complain to the Countryside Management Unit (see above). Some say that beef breeds are harmless and that bulls are quite docile when kept with heifers. I have put neither theory to the test and have always made an illegal detour to avoid a confrontation with a bull. Ironically, my brother-in-law and I were once chased by a herd of *cows* that, we kept telling ourselves, were just being playful! Be very careful if in charge of a dog: cows are fascinated by dogs and many accidents (some fatal) have occurred in the chaos that can ensue. Be even more wary of cows with young or new-born calves, and *never* walk between a calf and its mother. Watch out also for rams – sheep in general are a dim-witted breed and rams are usually just obstinate, but there have been many reported incidents and at least one fatality involving walkers.

ADLINGTON, POYNTON & DISLEY

Although geographically adjacent, these two areas provide an interesting contrast. Adlington is now almost entirely agricultural, while Poynton is a much larger settlement with many obvious clues to its industrial past.

The name Adlington is derived from Eadulvington – early Saxon for 'the place or farm of Eadwulf's people'. This is a good indicator to its agricultural origins. In the 19th century some small-scale mining took place, but not on the scale of nearby Poynton. Rather more important was the quarrying of stone – particularly the valued 'blue stone' from nearby Styperson, and brickmaking: several old brickyards are recorded on the OS maps and some derelict remains can still be found.

Poynton was originally part of the great sprawl of Prestbury, and became a separate parish only in 1871. It was very much the mining town of the area and, at one time, there were over fifty shafts spread over two miles. None of these was particularly deep – typically no more than

Poynton Pool *(photo: John Creighton)*

7

40m – but their output was sufficient for the Vernon family to make its fortune. This was aided by the arrival of the canal in 1831, and the railway in 1845. Each of these was good news for Poynton's coal industry, but the main impact of the railway was to permit the rapid and inexpensive transport of milk from Adlington, thus accelerating the return of Adlington to its agricultural base.

Whilst the Vernons were an important Poynton family, the Leghs of Adlington are more well-known locally. The family fortune also owes a great deal to coal mining, though the Legh family can trace its Adlington ancestry back to the 14th century. The most notable Legh connection is, of course, Adlington Hall. The Great Hall was built between 1450 and 1505, and the Elizabethan black-and-white addition dates from 1581. The gardens are quite beautiful, being the work of that amazing 18th century artisan, Capability Brown; well worth a visit while you are in the area. The seventeenth-century organ in the Great Hall is said to have been played by Handel. The hall is open to the public in August, Sundays to Wednesdays only, between 2pm and 5pm. See www.adlingtonhall.com for details.

Adlington Hall

The hall and gardens of Lyme Park are even more famous, not least for being the setting for the scene in *Pride & Prejudice* (1995) where Darcy emerges from a lake. The main entrance for cars is near to Disley, on the A6, though there is also a free pedestrian-only entrance from West Parkgate, near Pott Shrigley. The park covers 566ha (1400 acres) in which are included a superb children's playground, many waymarked trails and a large and well-established herd of deer. Although these attractions are known to local people, it is surprising how few have visited the hall itself. This was the home of the Legh family, but was acquired by the National Trust in 1947. The interior is sparsely furnished, but is worth seeing for its intricate pear-wood carvings. In 2010, opening hours from the end of March to the end of October were 11am to 5pm, Friday to Tuesday. For current information, phone 01663 762023 or visit the National Trust website at www.nationaltrust.org.uk.

The Middlewood Way

In the 19th century, the Macclesfield, Bollington and Marple railway transported coal and other commodities to and from Poynton. The railway closed in 1970 but the trackbed has been developed as the Middlewood Way – a linear route for walkers, cyclists and horse riders (in order of popularity). For details of the history of the railway, its demise and subsequent development, see: www.marple-uk.com/middlewood.htm.

The Walks

It is part of the charm of walks in this area that they almost always combine lush agriculture with the industrial past, a stately home – or all three! The terrain varies from pancake-flat to moderately hilly – particularly as you stride through Lyme Park. From here, you also get tantalizing glimpses of the real hills of the Pennine range to the east.

The walks range from six to twelve miles over moderately hilly ground. For a long, stimulating walk, tackle walk APD3 which has a good blend of interesting features and some first-class scenery.

Other Walks

In addition to the walks in this book, a free 'Green Walks' brochure for the area is available from local Information Centres or as a free PDF download from www.simonholtmarketing.com/GreenWalks.net/Contents.htm.

Walk: APD1

Adlington, Adlington Basin and Styperson Pool

Starting Point: Lay-by on A523 near the Legh Arms, Adlington SJ911804

How to get there: The start point is located mid-way between Poynton and Prestbury, near the crossroads with the minor road from Wilmslow to Pott Shrigley. Adlington railway station is very near to the start of the walk.

Map: OS Explorer 268 – Wilmslow, Macclesfield & Congleton

Length: 6½ miles

Grade: Easy/Moderate

Duration: About three hours

This varied walk combines pleasant rambles through meadows and woods, a stroll along a canal tow-path and a visit to one of the few lakes in the area. This variety more than makes up for the almost unavoidable one-mile stretch of road walking involved. Fortunately, the road is not a busy one.

Starting at the lay-by (1) on the A523 near the Legh Arms, turn left along Brookledge Lane (signed to Pott Shrigley) then, after a few hundred metres, turn right into Wych Lane (2). This road peters out into a track, taking you past Wych Wood.

'Wych' rhymes with the first syllable of 'lychee', not with 'witch', so the locals tell me, though there are also tales about a witch who used to live in this wood. One thing that is certain, however, is that Wych Wood is one of the prettiest bluebell woods around, but can now only be admired from the outside as it has been protected by barbed-wire fencing.

Staying with the main track, this eventually bends sharply to the right, at which point you go over a stile, and through a field to Harrop Green Farm (3). About 50m past the farmhouse, turn right at a stile (footpath sign) and walk under the electricity cables, keeping the hedge on your immediate right, until you are approximately half-way across the field. From here, turn left (signposted) to a stile which is near a large oak tree and to the right of a small wood. Cross this stile.

Styperson Pool, from the road to Pott Shrigley

Bear half-left, heading between the corner of an adjacent field and a large tree. Continue gently uphill past a marker to a stile, next to a gate in the top-left-hand corner of the field. Here, three stiles (if you include the 'gap' adjacent to the signpost) cross the Middlewood Way. The path in this next field is fairly obvious: it keeps to the right of a wood, and then leads to a bridge over the Macclesfield Canal. At the bridge, turn left, and join the towpath (4), keeping the canal on your right.

The towpath passes under a road bridge, and after a further 100 m, go through a stile on your left (5) and bear right across a field to a stile hidden in a dip in the top-left corner. Here, join a path where you again turn right towards a gate. At this point, cross the road to yet another stile on the left of the gate opposite. Springbank Farm (6) is on your left and a signpost points to Jepson Clough.

Walk along a well-made track until you reach a small wood with an attractive black-and-white house set inside it. Turn right at a signpost and, with the property on your left, circle around it until you join a path, which crosses a small bridge over a stream. Pass through a stile immediately after the bridge and head uphill, bearing slightly right and passing markers to a further stile 50m to the left of Jepsonclough Farm (7).

Small but interesting fact: landscape features (e.g. Jepson Clough) are often run together (e.g. Jepsonclough) when used in a farm name.

Turn left onto a tarmac drive. After about 50m, fork left and, after a further 50m, turn right at a T-junction. From here, continue on a tarmac track through a small wood, across the canal and through a caravan site.

At the end of this track, turn left just before Woodend Farm (8) and continue to another track, where you turn right and follow waymarks for a diversion to Adlington Basin (9).

This is a popular halt for pleasure craft – time for a few photographs and a breather before the uphill stretch of the walk.

You may or may not have made the diversion to the canal basin, but where the right of way meets (or met) the road, turn right along a track marked as a Private Road to Lockgate Farm (10). Note: this is *not* the first collection of buildings – the farm is at the very end of the track. Immediately beyond the farm, turn right at a stile, then across another stile and after 50m or so, cross the field at an angle of 45° towards the far hedge. Turn left here and, after 250m, with the hedge on your right, pass through a stile next to a gate and proceed along a grassy track to the main road. Turn right and have a rather boring time for a mile or so (actually, it's not too bad, and there's no easy alternative – but there is the excellent Coffee Tavern on the way). Turn left at the road junction (i.e. ignore the right turn to Adlington) and very soon you will find a footpath sign (11) on the right, leading towards Styperson Pool.

Follow the direction of the signpost, circling to the left of a scrubby area of gorse and bramble until you find a path on the right, slanting downhill. Eventually, pass the pool and go to a road, where you turn left towards Winterfold Farm. Before the farm, and immediately before a cottage, turn right along a path to the canal. Cross the canal and head towards Higher Doles Farm (12). A public footpath continues along a track and under the old railway (the Middlewood Way again) but this path is often waterlogged. Therefore, rather than using the tunnel, go to the Middlewood Way and turn left along it. After a couple of hundred metres, turn right at an exit signposted 'Holehouse Lane' and turn left to join a track. Continue along this track to a large house (13) now called 'Whiteley Croft' but marked as 'Oakdene' on the OS map.

From here, the directions must be followed carefully. Keep Whiteley Croft and its neighbour on your right as the track bends round to the right. Cross over a cattle grid and, keeping the hedge on your right, go

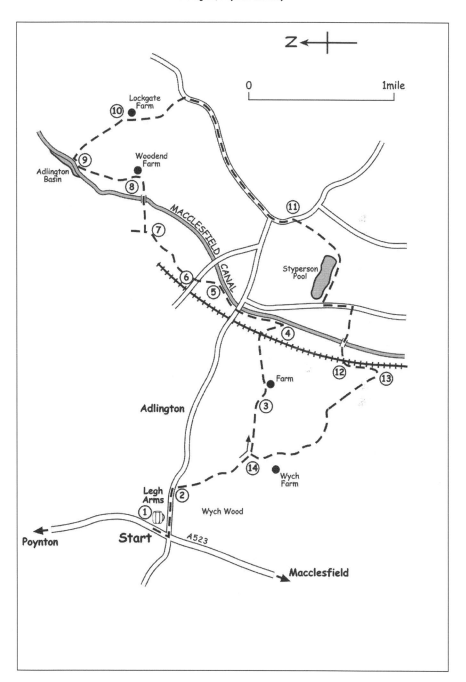

over a stile or the cattle grid in the top-right-hand corner of the field. Bear right in a due north-westerly direction, away from the track, and across the field to a waymarked stile. Cross this and the next one, in line with the house in front of you. Just before the house, swing left and walk alongside the hedge. Cross the stile by a gateway and go straight ahead (not due left or right – there are other paths here) to pass under the electricity cables. Then, keep the hedge on your immediate right and pass through the stile in the top corner of the field.

Turn left after this stile, follow the hedge on your left and cross a small plank bridge to another stile (there is *almost* a record number of stiles on this walk!). Then turn right, following the hedge with Wych Farm on the far left.

Nearly home now: cross another stile and walk almost straight across the field, heading slightly to the left. This brings you onto a track (14) which, if taken, leads left to Wych Farm, but you turn right, then left, and you're back at Wych Wood, almost where you started. Just keep walking back to Adlington.

Walk: APD2
Poynton, Higher Poynton, part of Lyme Park

Starting Point: Car Park on South Park Drive, Poynton SJ922840

How to get there: off the A523, a quarter of a mile from Poynton in the direction of Hazel Grove. The (unsignposted) car park is a few hundred metres along South Park Drive, almost opposite to Lakeside Drive.

Map: OS Explorer 268 – Wilmslow, Macclesfield & Congleton

Length: 6 miles

Grade: Moderate

Duration: About two and a half hours

This walk takes you through part of the old coal mining area of Poynton, over a disused railway line and along the Macclesfield Canal, each of which contributed to the area's past mineral wealth. All this is now long gone, but the remains are easy to find.

> If you want to read about the industrial archaeology of the area, the most useful publication is 'Poynton, A Coalmining Village' originally published by Macclesfield Groundwork Trust and available at www.brocross.com/poynton/conten.htm. Another walk (APD5) in this edition explores the area's industrial heritage and includes a visit to the Anson Museum; there is a small amount of overlap between the two.

Leave the South Park Drive car park (1) and turn left. After a few hundred metres, turn right at a T-junction, then pass through a waymarked gate on your left (2). The path goes straight ahead, passing a large pool behind trees on your right. Continue ahead, with a fence on your right. After a further 50m, bear slightly right – still following the fence – along a path towards a wood (3). The path is really more of a track, and is slightly elevated, being on the route of Prince's Incline, a 1:40 rope-hauled railway used for transporting coal from Higher Poynton down to a coal yard near the main road and (probably) to Poynton railway station. Soon, cross a track (noticing the brick-built culvert on the left) and continue up the incline to a display board that explains where the various inclines ran.

The Anson Pit, winter 1904. *(Reproduced by permission, the John Ryan collection)*

Continue to a road (4), which you cross and continue along Prince Road – a very minor byway. Cross Carleton Road and go over the bridge. Below is the Middlewood Way (see p9). The path continues towards the canal, just before which you see remains of buildings associated with the local mining activities. Turn right (5) at the canal and follow the towpath to bridge number 14 which you cross (6) and then carry on towards Barlow House Farm. Follow the official diversion alongside the boundary fence around the property. Cross a stile almost in the corner of a field facing you, being sure *not* to use the one next to a gate that leads off to the right. Having chosen the correct stile, continue in the same direction that you were travelling.

At the end of this large field, go over a stile (7) and turn left. After 50m or so, turn right over another stile and resume your previous direction of travel with a fence on your left. The Lyme Cage folly is now visible ahead and to your right.

At a farm track, turn left (8) and walk towards Middlecale Farm. Just before the farm, turn right and go along another track to the canal. Cross the canal bridge and immediately turn left between a pair of hedges (9). At the end of this track, turn left over a stile and head for Pool House

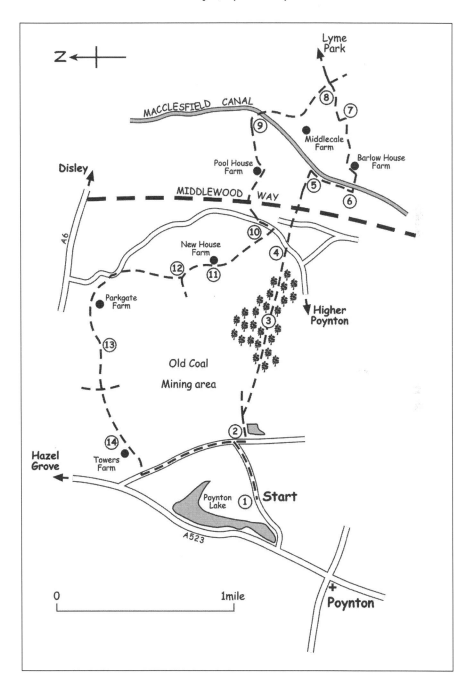

Farm. Bear right along a footpath before the farm, and soon join a road through a smart housing estate. Cross the Middlewood Way again and continue along a road (Pool House Road).

At the end of this road, turn left and walk along a busier road until just before a small layby with stables behind. Turn right at the footpath sign near to 'German Lodge' uphill on a track (10) that leads past New House Farm(11) – the much older buildings look interesting but neglected. After the farm and a clutch of communication masts, the track bends to the left and then, after a further 50m, turn right at a gate (12) from where there's a superb vista of Stockport. It looks quite nice from here! Walk through a large field, with a hedge on your right. Cross a stile into a wood and continue for about 20m to a T-junction of paths. Turn left and slant downhill on the right of way, heading gently downhill to the road through Norbury Hollow, where you turn left.

Walk along the road for about 50m and turn left again, along the drive to Parkgate Farm. Go through the farmyard and between various outbuildings towards a wood. Go through the wood, cross a stile by a gate (13) and follow a tractor path to Towers Farm (14). Continue past the farm and follow the waymarked path, being sure to spot the last waymark which leads off to the right, and onto a minor road (Towers Road). Turn left here and continue for half a mile or so, then turn right at South Park Drive and walk the last few hundred metres to the car park.

Walk: APD3
Higher Poynton to Furness Vale

Starting Point: Nelson Pit car park, Higher Poynton SJ945832

How to get there: From the centre of Poynton, follow Park Lane for almost a mile; keep left at the first major fork then fork right up Anson Road. Go over the crossroads by the Boar's Head and turn left into the car park – if the lower one is full, use the much larger higher one.

Map: OS Explorer OL1 – The Dark Peak Area

Length: 12 miles

Grade: Moderate/strenuous

Duration: Six hours

This fairly lengthy walk includes a good variety of attractions – a disused railway track, a canal, reservoirs, a stately home (with a herd of deer) – and a curiosity in the shape of the Dipping Stone, more of which later. There are fabulous views of Kinder Scout, Shutlingsloe and Bleaklow along the way.

We start from Nelson Pit car park. There's a visitor centre here, where you can find out about Poynton's history.

At the entrance to the car park, be sure to inspect the modern sculpture representing a pit-head winding gear, together with a representation of the 74 coal pits that once were so important to the prosperity of the area. Around here, there's also a pub (the Boar's Head), two cafés and a picnic site where the station used to be. For more information on Poynton's coalmining past, see walk APD5.

Turn left out of the car park (1) and walk up the lane, passing a group of houses called Mount Vernon (in deference to a coal baron). At the canal, turn right to walk along the towpath, heading south with the canal on your left.

After about five minutes, cross the canal at footbridge number 16, noticing the remains of a swing-bridge. The route leads diagonally to the right (2), away from the bridge, and along a well-trodden path punctuated by gates. Head toward the buildings of Green Farm on the

The Macclesfield Canal, near the start of the walk

skyline, passing Throstlenest Farm, almost hidden behind hedges on your left.

> 'Throstle' is Old English for song thrush; in the early 1800s, it was also the name of a spinning machine used to twist and wind fibres of cotton or wool continuously – it made a bird-like whistling noise as it operated!

Continue uphill and, eventually, turn right in front of Green Farm House (3). From here, follow the farm drive all the way to West Park Gate (4), an entrance to Lyme Park, which is on the left and is marked by a lodge, large gates and a notice regarding the park closing time – take note! Go through the pedestrian entrance and take the first right fork across the stream. Follow the left-most path uphill and continue with a deep clough away to your right and, soon, a fence on your left. Follow the fence uphill and, as the landscape opens up, you will see a building (5) ahead – a restored hunting lodge known locally as 'The Pepperpot' (see walk B2).

From the building, ignore the broad path through the trees on the left and the path heading down to the right; instead, take the middle path, noting the outline of Lyme Cage ahead. (Though often referred to as a folly, this was also a hunting lodge, much larger than The Pepperpot). Continue through the edge of the wood with a wall on your right and you

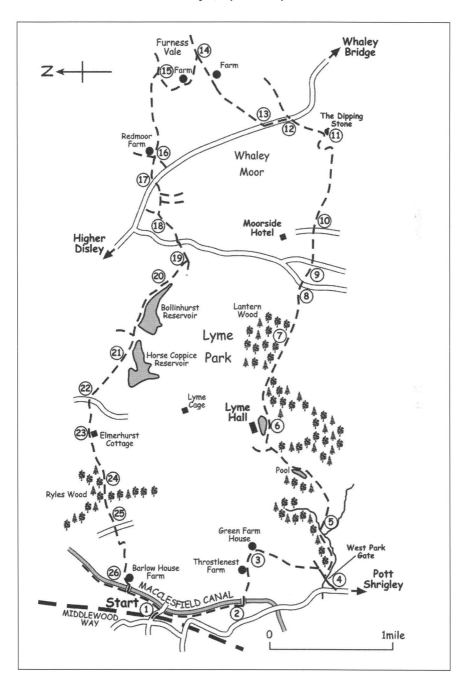

soon see Lyme Hall ahead. If you have not visited the hall, now could be the time to do it – but our route does not take us quite that far.

Join the main drive and cross a cattle-grid set between iron railings. Turn sharp right and follow a track (part of the Gritstone Trail) alongside a wall. Continue uphill to a stile in the wall. Cross this onto a clear path through the woods, and continue climbing to a white building (Bowstones Farm) with aerials around it. On reaching the stone boundary wall of the building, turn left *before* a stile and follow the wall until you come to the corner of Lantern Wood.

> Along the way, pass a commemorative plaque and toposcope erected to the memory of the children of Allan Monkhouse, literary critic for the *Manchester Guardian* from 1902 to 1932.

Turn right at a stone pillar just before the wood, and go over the stile in the wall. You can now see the Moorside Hotel and leisure complex ahead: your route lies a few degrees to the right of the hotel and takes you to a minor road (8). Cross this, go over a stile almost opposite and continue straight ahead, to the right of a large house on your left. Head downhill through an area that can be very boggy, finally bearing right to a stile leading to a road (9).

Cross this often busy road to a stile opposite. Go over this, head downhill and to your left to cross another stile and then a stream. The path now heads uphill – first through a large clump of gorse, then with a stream and fence on your right. Continue in this direction to cross a track (10), after which the path (signposted to Disley) continues uphill with a wall on your right.

At the far end of the field, a ladder stile crosses the wall, and the path becomes an obvious track, eventually crossing a further stile from where the outskirts of Whaley Bridge can be seen. Follow the obvious – and extremely pleasant – track as it contours around the moor. Eventually, you come to a high point from which you begin to drop down to a road, clearly visible ahead. Just before this, however, the Dipping Stone (11) is on your right, so be sure to make a small diversion to inspect it, even though it requires a small trespass.

> The stone resembles an old kitchen sink; the consensus is that it was used for cleansing coins in vinegar or some similar substance to avoid passing infection between parishes – a practice so famously carried out during the plague at Eyam. On a chilly December day, I used it to chill bottles of champagne to celebrate my 50th birthday!

A good use for the Dipping Stone!

Return to the main path and continue to the road, where you turn left (12). Walk along the road (be sure to ignore the first stile on your right) for about 300m, until you reach a gate on the right-hand side (13) – across the road there is another gate, which you do not cross, marked 'Private'. Instead, turn right and head towards a farm marked as 'Diglee' on the OS map. The buildings of Broad Hey Farm further ahead serve as a good direction finder. Continue down a clear track to the farm, through the farmyard gate and between the two main buildings, then along an attractive cobbled track.

Continue downhill for a few hundred metres to another farm track. Turn very sharp left here (14) and head towards Broad Hey Farm. The route runs to the left of the farm buildings (but not along the drive to the house) and along the farm track. Enter a small farmyard area and leave it through a gate on an overgrown concrete track.

Follow the track uphill to a barn (15) on the right. Turn left at a stile beside the gate facing the barn. The path goes into the field and remains parallel to the wall 50m or so on the right. Halfway across the field, turn left and head for a stile.

Cross this and continue in the same direction to a stile by a gateway. The path runs to the left of a fence, then a stone wall, towards Redmoor Farm (16). Cross the farm drive and go over a stile. The path bears left, slants uphill to the right of a stone wall, heads towards a stable, and then to a footpath signpost at a road.

Cross the road (17) and go over a stile; continue straight ahead and turn right across a stile near a prefabricated building. The path runs to the left of the wall from here, very soon crossing yet another stile to lead into a large field.

Go straight ahead, past a signpost in the middle of this field, and continue to the next stile. Ahead are two reservoirs, alongside which you will soon be walking. Veer left towards the junction of two walls (18), then carry on over a stile towards the road. Cross the road, join a signposted path and go straight ahead towards the wood. After a short distance, you reach a stile near a track and a signpost to Kettleshulme. *Do not follow this sign.* Instead, turn right (19) and follow the path signposted to North Lodge. The path runs to the left of a stream with attractive wooded banks. It crosses the stream by way of an embankment (20), and heads to the easterly end of Bollinhurst Reservoir. Follow the wall past this reservoir, then go alongside the Water Board access track towards Cock Head Farm (21). Skirt around the farm, go through a gate and cross the field facing you. Cross the stile next to a gate, leading to a track with 'Deep Lagoon' warning signs alongside.

Continue along the track, turning right at a T-junction (which otherwise would take you to the water treatment plant) towards Lyme Park. Turn left at the signed park gate and cross the main park drive (22). Go over a bridge, passing one cottage on your right and, soon, a second on your left. Cross a cattle-grid then, at Elmerhurst Cottage (23), follow the sign for Middlecale Wood and Middlewood.

The path eventually leads into a wood (24), down to and over a stream, and up a flight of steps. Cross a stile to leave the wood and continue straight ahead. This path crosses the drive (25) to Middlecale Farm and enters a field with a hedge on your right.

Continue straight ahead until you reach a stile. Turn left and, after about 60m, turn right at the first of a pair of stiles (do not cross the second one). Keep the hedge on your left and follow the waymarked path to the canal, past Barlow House Farm (26). Be sure to keep the house and its gardens on your left. Join a tarmac track, cross a bridge over the canal and turn left to walk along the towpath. In just a few minutes you are back at the start point – note that you can leave the towpath before the next bridge by passing through a gap on the right which leads directly to the car park.

Walk: APD4
Disley, Mellor Moor and Strines

Starting Point: public car park at end of Station Approach (next to the Ram's Head), SJ974845

How to get there: From any direction, find the traffic lights in the centre of Disley.

Map: OS Explorer OL1 – The Dark Peak Area

Length: 7½ miles

Grade: Moderate

Duration: Three and a half hours

This is a brisk walk with fabulous views. It passes through two golf courses, but a more interesting fact is that it is the most northerly route in this book. There are many possible variations, though this is probably the most scenic.

From the car park, walk back towards Fountain Square in the centre of Disley. Cross the main (A6) road at the traffic lights and go up Jackson's Edge Road (1). After almost half a mile of uphill walking, take the third turn right into Stanley Hall Lane (2), signposted to Disley Golf Club. Soon, you have excellent views of Mellor Moor on your right and, further away, Kinder Scout. I reckon this is the best way to see Kinder Scout – from as far away as possible! Continue on the drive to the golf course, with the clubhouse over to your right. Turn left to pass the partially black-and-white Stanley Hall on your right.

It was never a hall in the landed gentry sense, but it could be restored to its former glory.

Continue along a track for 400m, then turn right at a waymark. Walk downhill between stone walls and towards a wooded area. Where the track bends left (footpath sign) go straight ahead to the wood (3). Pass through the wood and across a stile, then keep to the right along a track, which soon becomes a minor road.

The chimney passed on your left (4) is from a disused bone mill; its flue went down to the mill in the small valley below – all to get a good draught!

Ignore the first set of footpath signs as you walk along the road, then turn right at a lane signposted to Mellor and Cown Edge (5). Go downhill to the Peak Forest canal, cross an impressive lift-bridge and turn left. Follow the towpath for half a mile or so, and turn right just before a road bridge. Go downhill to the main road (6), which you cross into Barlow Wood. Follow the main track and continue on a footpath through a wooded area, then walk alongside the River Goyt to an elegant stone-arch bridge. Go over this, turn left and then, after 150m, fork right at a stone stile with a sign to Mellor and Cobden Edge. Follow the track, thick with the scent and sight of balsam flowers in late summer, and keep right at the only fork until you reach a viaduct over the railway. Cross this and continue straight ahead into our second golf course of the day – Mellor and Towncliffe Golf Club (7).

Keep ahead, past a pond on your right then through patches of silver birch and a small copse. Follow the path through this to a sign pointing straight ahead to '14th Old Course' – whatever that is. Follow this general direction but keep close to the right-hand edge of the course with a large wood on your right. Pass and ignore a footpath sign to the Cown Edge Way, and continue to the end of the wood and a substantial pond. Turn left along a track, past a large corrugated shed and then head right, uphill (8), on a tarmac lane. Pass a car park (9) below and on the left, just before leaving the grounds of the club, then turn right along a quiet lane marked as a bridleway. Stride along here, soon passing the entrance to 'The Banks' on your left and continuing to a point where a right of way crosses the lane (10). Turn left, up a sunken but well-maintained path between stone walls. Keep left at a fork, then join a wide track that still heads uphill. This eventually becomes a tarmac lane which continues to a junction – you are now at the edge of Mellor Moor (11), and you can catch your breath to admire the view.

Turn right – again on a tarmac surface – with a sign to Higher Capstone Farm. Notice the large cross on your left, erected as a local community project. Walk *past* a property on the right (a cattery when last walked) and the lane soon deteriorates into a grassy track. Continue to a signpost where you turn right through a gateway – superb views of Kinder Scout are obtained from here (12).

From here, it's all downhill – except for a few ups! Go down a grassy track, pass a house, turn left along a tarmac track and then, where the tarmac bears right, go straight ahead and over a stile into a field with a wall on your left. Follow an obvious path, crossing a further stile and reaching a signpost. Fork right as indicated, passing to the left of what

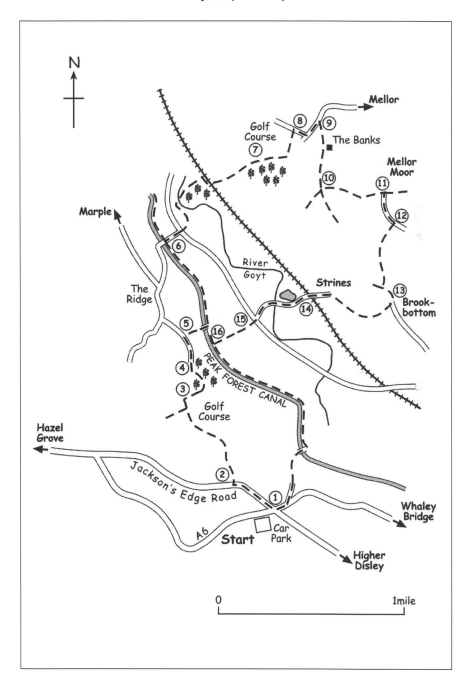

The dovecote at Strines

may be a large chicken shed. A few metres after this construction, turn right and go downhill to a stile, then turn left into the attractive hamlet of Brookbottom (13). Shortly after the Fox Inn, turn right along a track (part of the Goyt Way), soon going downhill with a stream in an increasingly deep ravine on the right. Pass under the railway and into the small but lively village of Strines.

Your route continues along a road, passing a remarkable dovecote in the middle of a lake (14) still used by the angling club established over fifty years ago for the workers at the Tootal fabric factory.

Cross the main road (15) and follow a track towards the canal, perhaps with a diversion along the way to the Woodland Trust site on the right. (This is an organisation very worthy of your support – take a look at its fantastic web site www.woodland-trust.org.uk and consider joining to support their excellent work.) Further up, cross a stile on the left just before the canal bridge (16) and then turn left to follow the towpath.

Continue alongside the canal, first passing a lift bridge and then arriving at a swing bridge (17), just after a house on your right. Cross the canal here, bear left and follow the track that eventually becomes Hagg Bank Lane, leading under the railway and back to the centre of Disley. Several pubs are available but, sadly, there is no longer a café.

Walk: APD5

Anson Engine Museum and the Macclesfield Canal

Starting Point: Nelson Pit Visitor Centre in Lyme Road, Higher Poynton. Map reference SJ940835

How to get there: From the centre of Poynton, follow Park Lane for almost a mile; keep left at the first major fork then fork right up Anson Road. Go over the crossroads by the Boar's Head and turn left into the car park – if the lower one is full, use the much larger higher one.

Map: OS Explorer 268 – Wilmslow, Macclesfield & Congleton

Length: 2½ miles or 3 miles

Grade: Easy

Duration: One to two hours, plus visit to museum

The Nelson Pit Visitor Centre is normally open daily, but you can phone 01625 573998 to be certain. It opened in March 1999 and has a considerable number of displays. Here, you can learn about the history of Poynton and surroundings. An even more important part of this walk is the Anson Engine Museum with its superb collection of memorabilia and mining machinery, including well over 100 oil and gas engines.

Full details, including opening times and special events, can be obtained from the museum website, **www.enginemuseum.org** or by phoning 01625 874426. Be sure to phone before your visit.

From the car park, walk downhill towards the crossroads and then carry on down Anson Road, first passing the waste disposal site and then a bungalow called 'The Anson'. Shortly after this, turn right along the wide track leading to the museum (1). After about 200m you reach the main entrance.

The museum is on the site of the Anson Colliery. In 1856, it yielded 51,000 tons of coal – just look at the size of the spoil tips as evidence of the productivity of this pit! At its peak, the total output for Poynton was over a quarter of a million tons of coal per year. By the early 1920s, this had fallen to around 100,000 tons and the last pit was closed in 1935.

Inside the Anson Museum

Walk out of the museum grounds and turn right along the track, away from Anson Road – conifers on the right, golf course on the left. At the road, turn left for a few metres then cross the road to Hawthorne Grove. At the end of this lane, turn left and continue for 150m. Cross a tarmac road to where there is a choice of footpaths. Take the left-hand one, the route of a railway that, interestingly, was always worked by horses.

After a little more than a quarter of a mile, cross a metal stile and reach a notice board describing the area; this is near to the Park Incline and the site of the Albert Pit (2). Loaded trucks were hauled up to here from Park Pits by a stationary steam engine. Turn right here, pass a pool on your left and walk through the wood and then follow the approximate route of an old railway. Cross three stiles and, after the third, go over a crosspaths and continue ahead. A few metres later, pass a pool on the right that was a reservoir for Park Pits. Then, cross a stile in the fence and continue in roughly the same direction.

Cross a main track to continue alongside a hedge and the remains of an embanked, but impassable, trackway. Cross a stile at the crooked corner in this field and continue alongside a fence. The levelled site of Park Pits (3) is on your left.

This was a very productive area: up to 180,000 tons of coal a year were mined at Park Pits from depths of up to 1000 feet (300m).

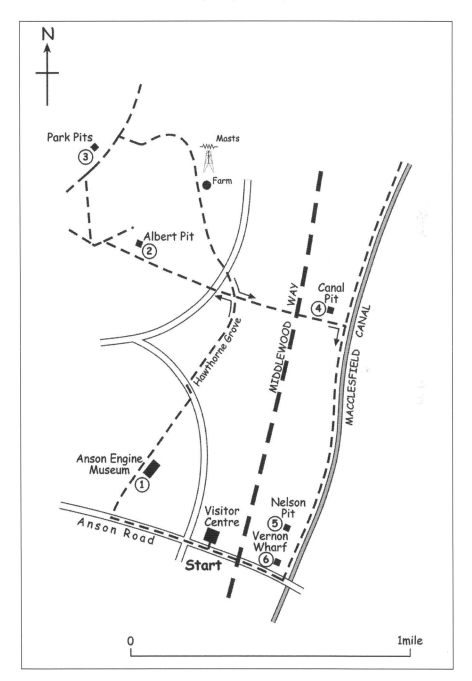

Continue through a plantation to a further fence and turn right. Head uphill, veering slightly away from the fence and head towards the communication masts. From here, follow the wide track that curves to the right to pass a house, then heads downhill to the road.

Cross the road, go through a stile with a stable on your right and then follow an elevated tarmac path. Turn left along Prince Road, continue over the crossroads with Carleton Road and cross a bridge over the Middlewood Way.

Continue to the Macclesfield Canal, which opened almost 40 years before the railway in 1831. On the skyline, you should be able to see Lyme Cage, the folly in Lyme Park. As you turn right onto the towpath, you are near the remains of Canal Pit (4).

> This pit that was never very productive, yielding only 7,691 tons of coal in 1879 and a meagre 1,543 tons in 1888. Its main purpose was to pump water from the various workings and it was known as 'Redlegs' because of its red pump rods which waved above the shaft when it was in operation. Nelson Pit was at location (5) and its coal was transported by canal to the mills of Bollington and Macclesfield; it produced 67,500 tons of coal in 1856.

Continue along the canal, passing under bridge number 14 and alongside the marina, often packed with boats of all shapes and sizes. Soon, cross a tiny hump-backed bridge over a spur from the canal: this is Vernon Wharf (6), where canal boats were loaded with coal from the pits.

> A rope-hauled tramway carried coal tubs from Anson Pit up to this wharf, which is why the pavement is so wide on the bridge over the Middlewood Way that you will soon be able to inspect. Remember to look at the stonework on the bridge parapet and you will see the grooves cut by the haulage rope.

Before leaving the canal towpath, you pass the small canalside shop (ice creams here) and turn right at the bridge over the Way, then down Lyme Road to return to the car park and visitor centre. More substantial refreshments are available just minutes away at the Boar's Head, on the crossroads, and 'The Coffee Tavern' just to the left of the pub. Note that there is another café of the same name just a mile or so away at Pott Shrigley!

ALDERLEY EDGE

This area has three distinct facets:

– the village itself, with an attractive range of restaurants and specialist shops to complement those of nearby Wilmslow.

– the residential area; as in Wilmslow, many large houses were built in the mid-19th century when the railway company offered a 'perk' of a first-class season ticket to and from Manchester for 20 years to anybody who built a house worth between £50 and £150.

– the surrounding countryside, based mainly on The Edge itself, on the way from the village of Alderley Edge to Macclesfield.

The Edge is owned by the National Trust, and this is the focus of the walks in this section. It draws visitors like a magnet, and on a Sunday afternoon is definitely not the place to be if you fancy a quiet stroll. Indeed, the volume of visitors is so high that erosion is quite a problem.

But, whenever you do visit Alderley Edge, be sure to call at the Visitor Centre, which is near to the main car park. This is open from Easter to October, and will give you an immediate insight into the geography and history of the area. There's also a tea shop, currently open weekends and Bank Holidays.

As most local people will know, there are two Alderley traditions you ought to know about: the mining industry, which is factual, and the legend of Merlin, which is entertaining but probably the product of a fertile imagination. The two are linked, however, as you will soon see.

The legend claims that a farmer from nearby Mobberley met a wizard-like man at Alderley Edge, whilst travelling to Macclesfield fair to sell his white horse. The old man offered to buy the horse, but the farmer refused, causing the 'wizard' to tell him that he would fail to sell the horse at the fair. When, later that day, the farmer returned with the unsold horse, our wizard character is said to have led him across The Edge, past Stormy Point to a rock which he tapped with his wand. Suddenly, a pair of iron gates was exposed, which opened into a cavern. They, with the white horse, entered to see several similar horses and their owners, all in a state of suspended animation and waiting for just one more horse to complete the 'army' which would be able to suppress some ill-defined uprising. The farmer was allowed to help himself from a pile of gold and then to leave – he being luckier than the army in waiting.

The view from The Edge

More definite, of course, are the mining traditions of the area. The caves are mostly man-made and the favourable exposure of copper- and lead-bearing seams has encouraged mining for many centuries. The Romans exploited the area and the discovery of a Roman coin in one of the shafts has been taken as evidence that mining took place in the 3rd to 4th centuries AD. But there were much more ancient mining activities than that. One of the most significant discoveries came in 1993, when a wooden shovel owned by local author Alan Garner was shown by carbon dating to be Bronze Age (approx 1750BC).

Most of the visible remains of mining that you can see nowadays date from around 1708 when a small but unsuccessful mine was begun by a Mr Abbadine, from Shropshire. Several other speculative mines were dug, but few were commercially successful. Copper ore was the main product, and the largest mines were Engine Vein, near the car park, and West Mine, on the other side of the road.

There have been attempts to open the larger caverns to the public, but these have failed to date. Groups, however, can visit some of the mines by arrangement with the Derbyshire Caving Club for a nominal fee. For detailed information about the mines and their history, go to www.derbyscc.org.uk/alderley.

The Walks

Our walks all begin at the main National Trust car park. As The Edge is perched so high above the surrounding plain, the beginning and end of any walk in this area has a modest amount of hill climbing. The two main walks in this section give you a fair contrast between the two sides of The Edge – one leading in the general direction of Mottram's fertile Cheshire farmland, and the other towards Nether Alderley, an area with many historical connections and a sprinkling of interesting buildings.

The track from the NT car park to The Edge

Walk: AE1
The Edge and The Hough

Starting Point: National Trust Car Park, Alderley Edge SJ860773. Note: this is a pay-and-display car park and the gates are locked at dusk – check the time before starting the walk.

How to get there: from Alderley Edge village, drive up Macclesfield Road (B5087); the NT car park is on the left, soon after the Wizard restaurant.

Map: OS Explorer 268 – Wilmslow, Macclesfield & Congleton

Length: 3 miles

Grade: Moderate (one steep climb).

Duration: One to two hours

This takes you around the edge of The Edge (!), along to the Armada Beacon, then to a super view across the Cheshire countryside and down to the flatter walking of The Hough. There's a fairly strenuous return route, past one of the many mines once worked for copper. Quite a varied walk for such a short distance.

Walk from the car park to the Information Centre (and tea rooms), then turn right and take the first turn left; immediately after this (NT sign and contribution box), fork left along on the narrower of two tracks, with a small car park on your left (1). Pass what appears to be a cast-iron water pump and, 100m further on, a disused mining area on the right. Continue ahead, still with the main road on your left, and keep left at a fork (where there is a bridleway to the right). Cross a main track and, after about 200m, climb a mound to the site of the Armada Beacon (2).

> This was erected in 1578 but the building which used to stand here was allowed to fall into disrepair, and in 1931 was destroyed in a gale. The mound is believed to be part of a Bronze Age burial site or 'barrow'.

From the beacon, retrace your steps to level ground, head left for a few paces and then right on an unmarked level track that curves to the left, passing a stone circle (the 'Druid's Circle') on the right. Soon you reach the Stormy Point viewpoint with views across Mottram, Prestbury and the outskirts of Bollington, all the way to the distinctive plateau of Kinder Scout, away on the horizon.

All that's left of the Armada Beacon – but what lies below it?

With your back to this superb panorama, turn right (almost north) along a wide unmarked track – so that you're still going in the same direction as before, if you had not stopped to admire the view. The path goes downhill to a dip, where you turn left down an often 'mushy' track. This slopes below the hillside for 100m or so to a T-junction, then makes a sharp hairpin left and continues alongside a field on the right. After a bit less than 100m, the track turns right and descends on a sunken path past stables and then a house until you reach the road (3), with a sign for 'Bracken Hill'.

From here, you can chop about a mile off the walk by turning right and walking along the road for about 200m to the point just after (7) in the text. For the complete walk, however, cross the road to join the drive to Saddlebole Farm. You are now in 'The Hough' – a lowland area between Mottram St Andrew and Alderley Edge that has mostly been agricultural. Many 'farms', despite their names, have been gentrified in recent years.

The area was not always entirely agricultural; Saddlebole is believed to have been a Bronze Age site of copper smelting – 'bole' is the old English word for hearth.

Continue towards the property but turn left over a stile at the end of the drive and walk along the edge of the field, with the hedge on your right. At the end of this, turn right and follow the next hedge as far as the road (4), where you turn right.

After a few hundred metres, turn right at the footpath opposite Brook Farm (5). Walk straight ahead – the path runs alongside the hedge after a hundred metres or so. Immediately after a pool on your left, cross the stile and turn right. Turn right again at the next stile (6). (A little-used path turns left here to Faulkner's Farm – this makes an excellent extension to the walk. Consult your OS map: you can easily follow this path, swinging round through Mottram Hall and back through Mottram St Andrew.)

For now, follow the path I suggested and continue with the hedge on your right. Cross the footbridge over Whitehall Brook and follow the path straight across the field as indicated by a waymark to a stile in the top-left corner. Follow the hedge (on your left), go over two more stiles and you will meet the road at a point to the left of Dickens Farm (7).

Cross the road and go through one of two stiles to start the return journey up to The Edge. In previous editions, I left the reader to their own devices from here but, with the maze of footpaths on the Edge, on reflection, that now seems unwise so here is a suggested route. Start walking uphill and, after about 200m, fork left at a large holly bush and continue on a wide track. This soon descends to a T-junction, where you turn right on a level track. Keep right at the next fork and climb the ever-steeper track which takes you above the entrance to Pillar Mine (now without its pillar) . This is worth a look – but I don't recommend venturing too far inside. From the mine entrance, continue uphill on a path that rejoins a track. Turn left and follow this to a T-junction with fields beyond. Turn right and head back to the car park, noting the Sutton Common communications tower away to the left, across the fields.

If you've timed it right, the tea shop could be open (weekends and bank holidays only!) – or maybe the ice-cream van will still be in the car park.

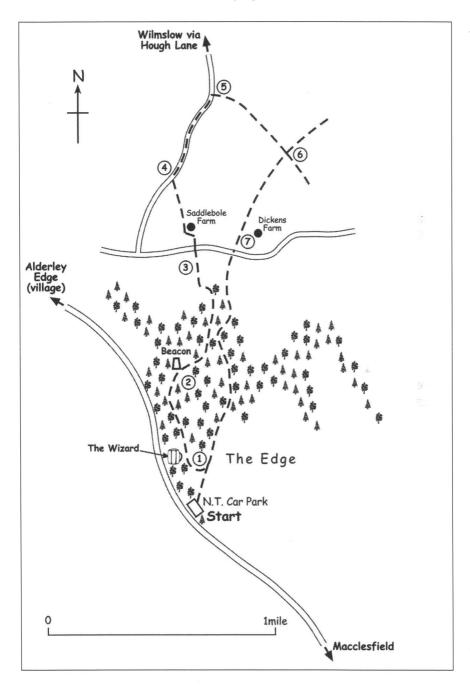

Walk: AE2
The Edge to Nether Alderley

Starting Point: National Trust Car Park, Alderley Edge SJ860773. Note: this is a pay-and-display car park and the gates are locked at dusk – check the time before you start the walk.

How to get there: see previous walk

Map: OS Explorer 268 – Wilmslow, Macclesfield & Congleton

Length: 6 miles

Grade: Moderate

Duration: Two and a half hours

This walk is not quite as popular as the previous one, though still well-walked and signposted, so you won't lose your way. It includes optional detors to Nether Alderley Church (St Mary's) and Nether Alderley Mill, to make for a surprisingly varied walk.

Turn left out of the National Trust car park (along the main road towards Macclesfield) and take the first turn right along Bradford Lane. Walk along the lane and around a left-hand bend where the road becomes Finlow Hill Lane. Continue as far as a sharp left-hand bend (1). Go straight ahead through a kissing gate and between wire fences. The tower on the skyline is at Croker Hill (Sutton Common) beyond Langley.

Follow the path, soon with just a single fence on your right and, as it starts to descend, spot the Jodrell Bank radio telescope away to your right. Cross a stile then turn right (2) at the road (Slade Lane) and go as far as a staggered crossroads (3). Carry straight on here, along the signposted bridleway to Jarman's Farm.

Mid-way between the first and second groups of buildings turn right at a kissing gate (4) and footpath sign. Follow the field boundary, cross a stile then follow an excellent stony track to a stile in a boggy area.

For years, this small area had been subject to flooding due to poor drainage. In May 2010, gates and a new track had greatly improved matters – just one small boggy area remained.

Continue straight ahead across the large field facing you, Cross the next stile and continue towards a farm, but turn right (6) before the farm gate. Go over a stile in the next corner of the field and follow the path to the left, soon alongside a small wood on your left.

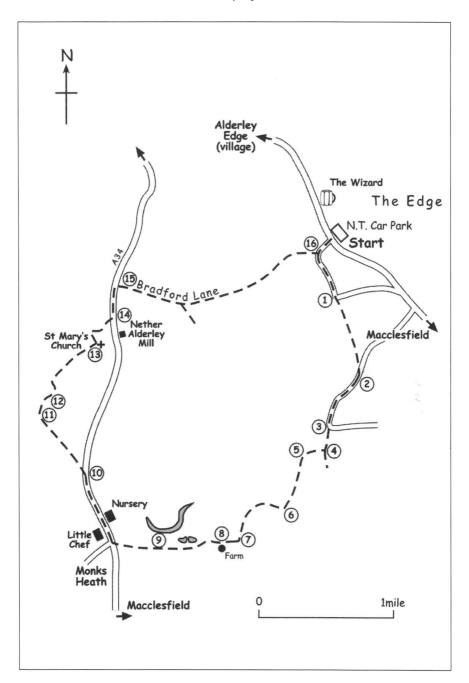

At a stile, fork right (waymark) and go diagonally across the field (in May 2010, this was surrounded by an electric fence). Your next stile, which is not easy to spot, is on the right, about 100m before the top-right-hand corner of the field (7). Cross this, another one after a very few metres and carry straight on towards farm buildings. Pass the buildings (8) and continue more or less ahead across a prairie-type field, catching sight of "The Serpentine" lake (9) and then parts of the Astra Zeneca complex on your right.

Enter the next prairie and continue ahead to a stile hidden away in the curve of the field edge – not quite on the official right of way. Cross this and continue to the main road. Turn right in the direction of Nether Alderley for about half a mile, then left (10) at a footpath sign shortly after Bollington Grange but before the roundabout for the Alderley Edge bypass.

A path takes you into a wood and over a stile. Continue through the wood to the next stile. Cross this and fork left across a field to a stile into another wood. When you emerge from here, turn right (11), pass Heawood House and carry on along a track.

Just before a bend to the left (12), with a house ahead, turn sharp right towards the entrance to a field, then sharp left along a footpath alongside a high conifer hedge. Continue to cross a small footbridge and a stile in quick succession. After this, keep straight ahead and cross the A34 Alderley Edge bypass by means of the footbridge – the only one over the new bypass, so we are in luck! Then, follow the path towards St Mary's (13) – the parish church of Nether Alderley, which also includes Great Warford and Over Alderley.

Short cut: if you do not have time for a visit to St Mary's or Nether Alderley Mill, turn left at the wall before the churchyard, pass through a stile and over a stream. From here, turn right, follow the stream (which flows from Nether Alderley Mill) and then turn left at a fence and follow it to the old A34. Turn left here (14) and continue to the final paragraph.

For the complete walk, including the church and mill, your next destination is St Mary's. Walk through the churchyard and on your right you will see the Stanley mausoleum – the Stanley family has a long association with the parish.

The church dates from the 14th century. Inside, there is an unusual gallery and an 18th-century 'Vinegar Bible', so-called because in the twentieth chapter of the Book of Luke, the typesetter had set the page-head for the parable of the vineyard to read 'The parable of the vinegar.' Not as bad as

Nether Alderley Mill

the 'Wicked Bible' of 1632 in which the seventh commandment reads "Thou shalt commit adultery". The church is open every Sunday afternoon 2.00pm to 4.30pm from Easter Day to the end of October and also on Bank Holiday Mondays. For further information and up-to-date information, see the website: www.stmarysalderley.com .

After your visit, walk from St Mary's along Church Lane and turn left along the old A34 towards Wilmslow. On your right is **Nether Alderley Mill.**

This is a working, water-powered corn mill lovingly restored by a mill enthusiast and now in the care of the National Trust. It is only open for group visits, by appointment. Phone: 01625 445853.

From the mill continue along the main road for about 200m towards the village of Alderley Edge to point (14) on the map.

Whether you took the short cut or the scenic route, this is the way back: after a quarter of a mile along the old A34, turn right ar Bradford Lane (15). After about half a mile, fork left and continue to a road. Turn left here (16), then left at the main road, and you're back at the car park.

Walk: AE3
The Edge and Over Alderley

Starting Point: National Trust Car Park, Alderley Edge SJ860773. Note: this is a pay-and-display car park and the gates are locked at dusk – check the time before you start the walk.

How to get there: see walk AE1

Map: OS Explorer 268 – Wilmslow, Macclesfield & Congleton

Length: 4 miles

Grade: Moderate

Duration: One and a half hours

This walk covers some of the same ground as walk AE2, but it is substantially shorter and ideal for a summer's evening.

Follow the directions for walk AE2 as far as the end of Slade Lane (3). This time, turn left and, after about 200m, turn right (4) at a stile signposted to Wrigley Lane. Go straight ahead, over two footbridges, then at the next stile (5), keep left and follow the fence until you meet the road, where you turn right.

About 200m before St Catherine's church, with its unusual octagonal tower, turn right along a drive opposite to a cottage. Keep going straight ahead, through the farm – do not fork right – until you reach the next farm drive (7), where you turn left.

Follow the drive until you reach Bradford Lane (8), the cobbled lane that began at point (15) on map AE2. Turn right and follow the lane back to the road (9), where you turn left, then left again to arrive back at the National Trust car park.

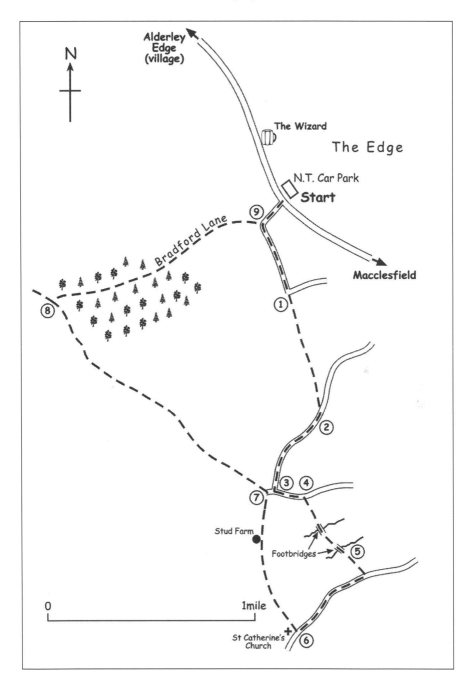

N

Alderley
Edge
(village)

The Wizard

The Edge

N.T. Car Park

Start

⑨

Bradford Lane

Macclesfield

①

⑧

②

③ ④

⑦

Stud Farm

Footbridges

⑤

0   1mile

St Catherine's
Church

⑥

Walk: AE4

Alderley Edge, Hare Hill and Bradford Lane

Starting Point: National Trust Car Park, Alderley Edge SJ860773. Note: this is a pay-and-display car park and the gates are locked at dusk – check the time before you start the walk.

How to get there: see walk AE1

Map: OS Explorer 268 – Wilmslow, Macclesfield & Congleton

Length: 4½ miles

Grade: Easy

Duration: Two hours

This is an easy stroll using the National Trust permissive path from Alderley Edge to Hare Hill. The best time of the year is late May to early June, so that you can visit Hare Hill, with its walled garden and impressive collection of azaleas and rhododendrons. (Open early April to the end of October. Daily for part of May when gardens are at their best; small admission charge. Go to www.nationaltrust.org.uk for current details.)

Cross the field from the car park (1) and join the main track that leads towards the Edge. Leave the track through a gate on the right and head to Edge House Farm, between two wire fences. Cross a stile at the farm and head downhill – there is a fine view of Shutlingsloe away to your right. At the very bottom of the hill, there is a stile leading left to the unspectacular but pretty waterfall in Waterfall Wood. Worth the small diversion.

The main route is straight ahead, the path again being between wire fences. Turn right after the next stile, walk alongside the field boundary, then turn left to the gentrified buildings of Hill Top Farm (2). At the end of the drive, turn left beyond the buildings, then almost immediately right and up a flight of steps signed to Hare Hill into Daniel Wood.

The route from here to Hare Hill is clearly waymarked, with the walk through the wood being a pure delight – mixed woodland rather than the curse of the conifer. Emerge from this wood and follow the field edge to the next plantation, Alder Wood. Follow the path through here and – just before the end of the track – turn right across a bridge and follow the Hare Hill signs to the lake (3), a popular picnic spot.

Next stop is Hare Hill gardens (4) – see details at the start of this walk. After your visit, cross the car park and walk along the main drive from

Alderley Edge

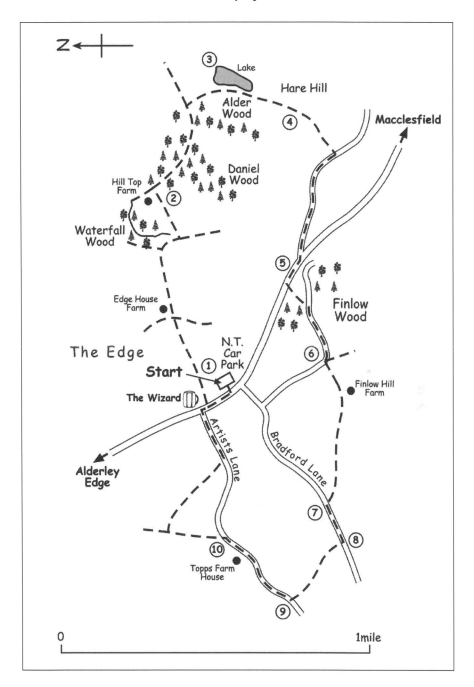

47

Entering Hare Hill

the gardens towards a minor road. Either cross a stile to the road and turn right or, immediately before the main gateway, turn right along the concessionary footpath parallel to the road, before rejoining it.

Continue to the main Alderley-Macclesfield road and turn right (5). After 100m, turn left (footpath sign) and follow the track through Finlow Wood, then turn right onto a minor road. Where this bends sharply to the right (6), carry straight on along a track to Finlow Hill Farm.

Cross a stile before the buildings, then carry on in the direction you were walking. After 200m, bear right alongside a line of trees to a pair of stiles. Cross these and follow the waymark to walk alongside the wood on your left, then cross an intriguing stile with four large, round stones that serve as steps. Continue across three more stiles to a wide, stony track (Bradford Lane). Turn left here (7).

Walk along the lane for 200m, then turn right at a stile just past a bungalow on your right (8). Follow the path with the hedge on your right to another stile. Cross this, then keep the hedge on your left until you reach a road (Artists Lane) where you turn right (9).

Continue uphill, passing the 17th-century Topps Farm House. To avoid too much tarmac: after a further 100m or so, turn left (10) and, after a similar distance, right at a gate leading to a path below Artists Lane. The path rejoins the lane, crosses it, and continues above and parallel to it – all the way to the Wizard and the car park. The tea room is open weekends and Bank Holidays – and there's usually an ice-cream van too!

BOLLINGTON

The first thing that strikes a visitor to the town of Bollington is its length – some 2.4 miles to be exact. After that, you notice the mills, an amazing number of public houses and lots of small shops. The whole atmosphere is more typical of a small town in Ireland than a Cheshire village.

Bollington had its roots in cotton, unlike the nearby silk town of Macclesfield. The last major employer in the cotton industry around here was Shrigley Dyers (slogan: "We live to dye!") but now there are mostly smaller enterprises and most of the mills have been converted to offices, light industrial purposes and apartments. Bollington is enjoying quite a revival as many properties are modernised and young people move into the town. There is live music in some of the pubs and a programme of cultural events staged in the Arts Centre.

Surprisingly, there are few sources of information about the town. The publications that I once knew about have long been out of print, and the Groundwork Trust Discovery Centre closed during 1996. The library is a good source of information and has copies of relevant publications. The town has its own website, www.happy-valley.org.uk.

There are several distinctive features in Bollington. The old railway viaduct and the Macclesfield Canal aqueduct both span the main street, and 'White Nancy', a monument at the end of Kerridge Hill, can be seen from miles around. For such a popular monument, hard facts about it are difficult to come by. One thing that's certain is that it was erected by the local Gaskell family to commemorate the victory at Waterloo, and it was originally an open shelter – since bricked up due to vandalism and decay. The origin of its name is, however, difficult to trace; it may refer to 'White Ordnance', or to a member of the Gaskell family. The one I prefer is that it was the name of the horse used to haul the construction materials up the hill!

Bollington is also the most popular place to join the Middlewood Way, a level route for walkers, cyclists and horse riders based on the track bed of the former railway – see page 9.

The Walks

Due to the excellent hilly terrain, most of the walks in this section fall into the moderate/strenuous category. Anybody wanting to do some 'real' walking should start here! A publication that could be of interest is

High Street, Bollington

'Walks Around Bollington' – a pack of booklets prepared for the 1980 Bollington Festival. Unfortunately, only a reference copy is available in Bollington library (Tel: 01625-573058). They also have a copy of 'Bollington – Cotton Town' available for loan. More recently, a series of 'Nostalgia Trails' leaflets has been produced by Bollington Drop-In Centre.

If you only have time for a short walk, there is now a public footpath to Nab Head, a magnificent viewpoint (and site of an ancient round barrow) on the outskirts of the town (SJ940788). This was due, in particular, to the untiring work of Bill Shercliffe and his colleagues in the East Cheshire Group of the Ramblers' Association, and Cheshire County Council (and no thanks at all to the landowners concerned).

Walk: B1

Ingersley Vale, Rainow and Swanscoe Hall

Starting Point: near the Cotton Tree pub, Ingersley Road, Bollington SJ940779

How to get there: Turn into Ingersley Road between the New Con club (previously the Turners Arms) and bus turning area. Park considerately.

Map: OS Explorer 268 – Wilmslow, Macclesfield & Congleton

Length: 6 miles

Grade: Moderate

Duration: Three hours

From your starting point, walk up Ingersley Road and, at the Poachers Inn, turn right down Mill Lane (2). The lane eventually narrows to a stony track and you soon turn left to pass a small row of cottages. Just at the back of the last cottage, and before a factory, turn left to climb stone steps, and go into a field (4). The path goes uphill and bears right, taking you past a wooden fence towards a wall on your left.

Look out for a combination of steps and a stile in the wall. Cross the stile (4), turn right and, after about 30m, turn left onto a wide grassy track leading uphill towards a set of gates.

Cross over the main drive of Savio House. Until the 1970s, this was Ingersley Hall Farm, but is now a retreat and conference centre run by the Salesian religious order. Continue along a wide, raised track towards a small wood (keep it on your left) then go through a kissing gate to a stony track (5). Turn immediately right after a step stile and right again to cross a stile with a Gritstone Trail marker and walk downhill, with a wall on your right.

> Long ago, this path was used by the men and women who walked to Bollington every day to work in the mills. It still has some of the original stone steps and paving.

Climb uphill to pass a white-painted house. After two stiles, you will find a third stile almost immediately on your right. Cross this but then turn left and continue on the right of the wall in roughly the same direction as before – i.e. do not walk downhill. On your right, as you pass through this field, you will see the White Nancy monument at one end of Kerridge Hill.

Continue to the end of the field. Go over a stile and walk straight ahead to cross a stile in the far-left corner. After entering this next field, cross a stile half-way along the opposite wall. The next stile is in the far-right-hand corner – squeeze through this and turn left towards Rainow, passing through two more stiles and down a stone-slabbed slope. On your right, you will see the lake and gardens of Hough Hole House, complete with its Victorian Allegorical Garden and stone plaques along a path representing the story of 'A Pilgrim's Progress'.

The gardens are currently open on the late May Bank Holiday and August Bank Holiday Mondays and to groups by prior arrangement at other times – phone 01625 573251 for details.

You soon reach a minor road. Turn right here (6). After 100m, turn left up steps (7) into a field. Keep to the right and head downhill, then cross a stile and two footbridges over streams. From here, head steeply uphill, roughly parallel to power cables on your right, heading for a gap in the trees at the top of the hill (8). From the top of the hill, you have a choice:

For a short walk: turn right and walk along the ridge to the White Nancy monument, commemorating the Battle of Waterloo. On your way, you will have a particularly impressive view of your outward route. From White Nancy, continue straight ahead to drop straight down to Chancery Lane and join the long walkers near the end of this description where it says "**Long and short walks join here:**".

For the complete route: carry on over the hill, then turn left alongside a wall and head steeply downhill to a road. Cross the road and turn right (9) along the wide track to Endon House. After 200m, and *before* the buildings, take a sharp left hairpin alongside a wide steel gate (10). After a few minutes, cross a stile beside a wide wooden gate. From here, ignore the OS map as there have been major changes and a permissive path provided, pending an official diversion. This is the current best route: cross a stile by the wooden gate, then turn left through a gate marked as "Permissive Path". Follow this across a field and cross the drive of Swanscoe Farm. The diversion continues, taking you through a gate and back onto the drive and then, after just a few metres, turns right through another gate to a flight of steps. At the bottom of the steps, the diversion turns left alongside a wall and emerges onto the drive to Lower Swanscoe Farm, from where you continue for half a mile to a road.

Turn right here and pass the entrance to Swanscoe Hall (11), keeping to the right along Swanscoe Lane. After 200m, bear right down a road

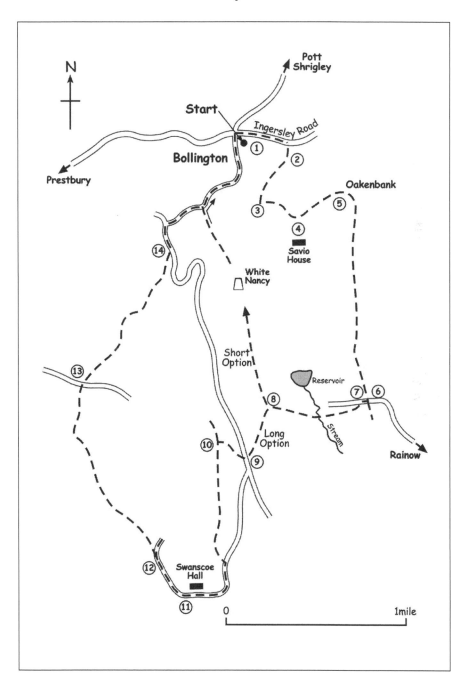

N

Pott
Shrigley

Start

Ingersley Road

Bollington

Prestbury

① ②

Oakenbank

③ ⑤

④
Savio
House

White
Nancy

⑭

Short
Option

Reservoir

⑬

⑧ ⑦ ⑥

Long
Option

Stream

Rainow

⑩

⑨

⑫ Swanscoe
Hall

⑪ 0 1mile

White Nancy

signed as a 'dead end' and, after about 100m, enter the private drive (12) signed to 'Woodlands, Woodend and Shrigley Fold'. After the second property, fork right on a signed footpath. Pass buildings on your left and follow the waymarks downhill. Continue towards a ruined barn, before which you turn left, then pass to the right of an old mine shaft. Go straight ahead on an obvious track to a small pool by a gate. Continue to the right of the hedge, and follow the waymarks to walk between two pools to the opposite stile.

Along the way, you may notice numbered plaques nailed to stiles and other locations. These relate to 'Nostalgia Trails' developed by the Bridgend Centre, a community cooperative based in Bollington. For more information, visit http://tinyurl.com/cpt8kv.

Cross a track, another stile, and bear right to follow the path to the left of yet another pool and continue to the road (13). Cross the road and walk to a small bridge across a stream. On your far left is the canal and ahead is the old Adelphi cotton mill. Bear slightly right from the bridge and keep the stream on your right as you pass through a succession of gates. Keep following the waymarks as you continue ahead until you reach a bridge over a stream. Bear right after this and pass through two kissing gates to cross a wide track; as you cross the final field, you can see the Hollin Hall Hotel to your left and you eventually join a road (14). Go left, walk along the road and turn right into Chancery Lane.

Long and short walks join here: continue along Chancery Lane, down Lord Street, along Church Street, and back to the starting point. A few years ago, you would have passed the premises of Shrigley Dyers (slogan: "We Live to Dye") – but the company closed in 2000 and the land has been used for housing development.

Walk: B2

Bollington to The Bowstones

Starting Point: lay-by, Spuley Lane SJ945782. Just outside the eastern outskirts of Bollington and officially in Rainow.

How to get there: Turn into Ingersley Road between the New Con club (previously the Turners Arms) and bus turning area; pass the Poachers Inn, bear left at the fork signposted to Pott Shrigley and the lay-by is on the right.

Map: OS Explorer 268 – Wilmslow, Macclesfield & Congleton

Length: 9½ miles

Grade: Strenuous

Duration: Four and a half hours

Starting on a historical note, the lay-by recommended for parking is in front of what used to be The Cheshire Hunt, an inn dating from the 1700s that was the focus for scattered farming communities for the buying and selling of livestock. Sheep and cattle were taken here along ancient drove roads – some of which are used on this walk. The pub closed some years ago, together with the nearby late-lamented Country Café – both for residential development.

The walk to Bowstones is a popular one for keen walkers. The suggested outward route is mainly based on moderately well-surfaced tracks, giving a fairly mud-free walk – the same cannot be guaranteed for the return section! Apart from seeing the Bowstones, a fair portion of Lyme Park is included in this exhilarating walk.

Leave the lay-by (1) and walk up the lane called Hedge Row – in springtime the verges here are a mass of wild flowers; continue uphill, ignoring the Gritstone Trail footpath marker on your left – you will return by that route. After about 5 minutes, pass an entrance guarded by a variety of stone animals and soon you are heading downhill (2) and generally to the left, towards a house. Go through the gateway, down the steep path and over Mellow Brook (3), which joins Harrop Brook on your left. Do not go over the second footbridge – instead, turn right (Gritstone Trail marker) to go uphill again. The path soon joins a more clearly defined sunken track, passing between rows of bushes and trees.

Along this track, look out for wooden 'musical' instruments and a pleasant signposted viewpoint just off-route – parts of Bollington's 'Nostalgia Trails' initiative. Ignore all side turns until you reach a prominent fork (4). Take the left fork down to Black Brook, then head slightly right and across the brook to a stile. Go over this and follow the track uphill with a boggy area to your left. As you climb the slope, the bogginess dries out to reveal a sunken path; keep this on your left and bear right (5) towards a wall. Continue towards farm buildings, then bear left at a signpost and head towards a ladder stile (6) along a route that now keeps you away from the farm itself. Cross the stile and keep the wall on your left, as far as the road. Do not use the farm drive.

At the road (7), turn left, then almost immediately right along a track (Gritstone Trail) leading directly to the Bowstones. Along the track look out for the toposcope (8) (signposted, on your right) – a metal plate indicating the locations of surrounding hills and other prominent features.

Continue towards the prominent white house (Bowstones Farm) with communications masts dotted around – almost as intrusive as a small wind farm. Pass the house and make a minor diversion to inspect the Bowstones (9).

These are believed to be the shafts of late-Saxon crosses; the cross-heads are said to be in the courtyard of Lyme Hall and their bases are in Disley churchyard. The shafts were probably removed to their present location to be used as boundary stones. There are more fanciful tales that they were used for stringing bows, sharpening arrowheads or for devotional purposes. Take your pick.

From the Bowstones, retrace your steps by a few paces and cross a ladder stile into Lyme Park. From here, you could well see some of the large number of deer in the park. Follow the path towards Knight's Low (10), the large wooded area. When you reach it, cross over a ladder stile into the wood and turn left. Follow an obvious track through the wood with the wall to your left. At the bottom left corner, leave Knight's Low over another ladder stile, cross a water channel, go down a few steps then go right and keep a wall on your right.

Follow the main track until you reach a building restored by the National Trust.

Known locally as The Pepperpot, but now called Paddock Cottage, this 17th-century hunting tower is worth a diversion. It was a smaller version of Lyme Park's 'cage' – a place from where the gentry and their ladies could observe stag hunts.

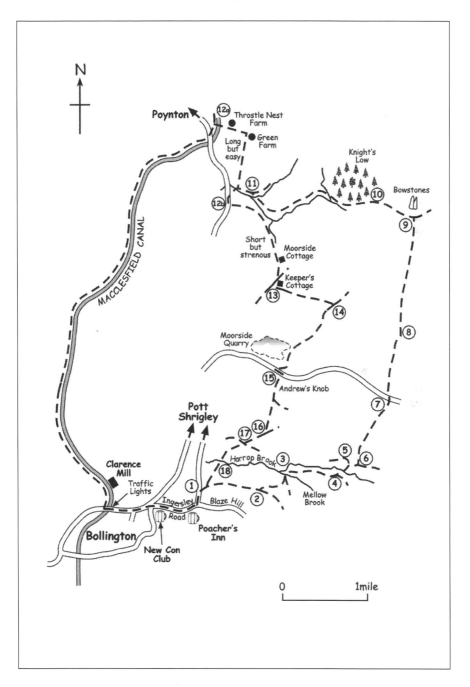

From here, continue in the same direction as before. Soon, a path starts to wind downhill, and heads through bracken until you reach a wide track by a stream (11). Turn left here and continue to West Parkgate, marked by a lodge and, of course, a gate.

> For future reference, this is a convenient – and free – rear entrance to Lyme Park; there is a small amount of car parking space – also free – on Shrigley Road (the minor road from Pott Shrigley to Higher Poynton.)

Immediately after leaving West Parkgate, you have a choice:

Easy-peasy (but longer) route: turn right and walk along the lane. After a few minutes, a path bears right over a ladder stile; ignore this and continue on the main track, over a cattle grid. Continue for a few hundred metres and cross a second cattle grid, heading towards Green Farm. The right of way is signed as continuing immediately in front of the buildings, but a newer track bends away to the left to join a hedge-lined track (and the right of way) heading downhill towards Throstle Nest Farm. Cross a stile on the left before this next farm, go right at the next stile, and continue along a well-used path. Alongside, in the summer, there is a glorious display of wild roses. Join the Macclesfield Canal at a bridge (12a). Cross the bridge and turn left, heading for Adlington and Bollington – no further instructions are necessary. (**Note:** do not be tempted to join the canal by walking along the road towards Poynton from West Parkgate; it is slightly shorter, much less pleasant and you have to walk through a *narrow, dark and dangerous tunnel*.)

Very eventually, you reach the outskirts of Bollington and Clarence Mill – now apartments and various enterprises. There are plans for a bridge over the canal to the mill (and The Chilli Jam café!) but until that happens, go down a flight of stone steps to the traffic lights and make your way back to the car.

Connoisseur's route: this is shorter and more scenic – but hillier. Turn left out of West Parkgate and walk along the lane until you reach the tiny Methodist church (12b).

> Note the spelling in the plaque above the door: New Connexion Chapel, 1851.
> 'New Connexion' was formed in 1797 as an offshoot of Wesleyan Methodism

Turn left here, along the track to the right of the chapel and continue, passing between the first two cottages you reach. The track becomes a path and generally follows a fence, then a wall – keep this on your immediate left, as it will enable you to find the stiles.

As the wall dips away downhill, head right along a very well-defined path. As you head across open moorland, Moorside Cottage will be seen to the left, and white-painted Keeper's Cottage ahead and slightly to the right. Head for the stile in the top-right-hand corner of the field – turn right, then left after Keeper's Cottage (13). Walk uphill alongside the wall, to a stile at the very top of the hill. Cross this and walk straight ahead, downhill. Just before the path levels out (after less than 50m), turn right (14) and walk along a fairly obvious grassy track to the road – a distance of about half a mile. Note the numerous capped mineshafts along the way –

Rebuilt packhorse bridge on the Gritstone Trail

reminders of small-scale coalmining in the area.

Turn left at the road, walk uphill for about 80m then turn right at the stile (15). Walk alongside a wall and then, at the top of the hill, continue in the same direction to walk alongside the next wall. At the first gate you encounter turn right (16) and head downhill with a wood on your right and a wall on your left.

Where the path joins the farm drive, cross the drive (17) and continue downhill in the same direction you have just travelled, keeping a 45-degree angle with the farm drive and dropping below the farm buildings. Continue over minor streams and go through a prominent gap in the stone wall above and to the right of a larger stream bed. Continue from here downhill to a reconstructed packhorse bridge (18), which you cross. Carry straight on and slightly left to go over the hill and to a stile leading directly onto Hedge Row – almost where the walk started. Turn right down the lane to return to your starting point.

Walk: B3
Big Low and Berristall Dale

Starting Point: Church Street, Bollington SJ939778

How to get there: Drive through Bollington to the bus turning area at the bottom of Ingersley Road. Church Street is to the right of the New Con Club. Park considerately.

Map: OS Explorer 268 – Wilmslow, Macclesfield & Congleton

Length: 4½ miles

Grade: Moderate/Strenuous

Duration: Two and a half hours

This walk includes the some of the most scenic surroundings of Bollington: Ingersley Vale, Big Low and Berristall Dale. Add to this an insight into Bollington's industrial past, and you have an ideal afternoon or summer's evening walk.

Begin by walking along Church Street past St John the Baptist church towards the smart apartments facing you (1). Turn left into Ingersley Vale and walk past the townhouses that replaced Shrigley Dyers, alongside the mill pool on your right, and the bowling green on your left. After this, continue past a series of nondescript industrial buildings until, where you walk below an iron aqueduct, you reach the stone-built remains of Ingersley Vale Mill.

> This housed the second-largest waterwheel in Britain (after the one at Laxey, Isle of Man) but there was a disastrous fire in 1997. Read more about it at www.happy-valley.org/ingersley.htm

About 50m or so after this mill, cross a stile (2) into a field. Go over the bridge and follow the grassy track (part of the Gritstone Trail) straight ahead, then uphill and to the left. Parts of the path, you will notice, are roughly paved – a common feature of many paths around here that were used by millworkers from outlying villages. Continue uphill, passing the old Ingersley Hall on your left.

> Once the home of the Gaskells, who built White Nancy, the hall is now called Savio House and is used by the Salesian religious order.

Onwards and upwards through stiles, and soon you see the

Big Low from Blaze Hill, on the outskirts of Bollington

prominent hump of Big Low facing you. Eventually, you reach a wide gateway where there used to be an adjacent stile (3). Cross the gate, or the stile if it is ever reinstated, and turn right along the farm track (Oakenbank Lane). After about a quarter of a mile, and before you reach the highest point on this track, turn left through a gate (4). Although unsigned, this is easy enough to find – there is another gate almost opposite and the gateway that you go through has a right-hand gatepost with three equally spaced holes through it. Walk into the field and keep the wall on your left. The footpath is a well-defined track leading to Crofts Farm. When you reach the farm, go through the farmyard and turn left (5) along the very minor road past Big Low.

This is on private land, but it is worth noting that Big Low may have been the location of an Iron Age hillfort. The name may seem odd but 'low' is Anglo Saxon for 'hill' and an alternative name is Great Low. Coal was mined on the south side of this hill in the 19th century – helping to satisfy Bollington's demand for power in its industrial past.

As you continue along what is becoming a stony track there are, on your left and just beyond the highest point, excellent views of Kerridge, White Nancy and Bollington. Further away, Alderley Edge is clearly visible. Do not upset the farmers by straying into the fields to admire the view – keep to the path.

At a T-junction with another track (6), turn right and, ignoring side turns, continue to the road. Turn left then almost immediately right, through a gate (7). From here, carry straight on down a track, ignoring the fork on your left. As the track continues downhill, you will see a stone-built property on your left (8). Immediately after this, cross the stile on your left (signpost to Bower Clough and Spuley Lane), turn immediately right and continue downhill – the path goes over a stile to the right of a large holly bush and continues to the left of a fence and the stunted remains of an old hedge. At the end of the fence/hedge, cross a field and head towards the farm building, where there is a stile in the fence (9). Cross this and turn right through a gate to head downhill to two footbridges in the quintessentially English setting of Mellow Brook – see picture on cover. From the second footbridge (a single-slab 'clapper') head uphill and to the right towards a stile. Go over this and continue a short distance to a vehicle track (10), where you turn left.

Continue winding uphill along the track until you pass through a gateway with a wood converging from your right and farm buildings straight ahead. What follows is the only tricky part of the walk – so be careful. Almost exactly half way between the gate and the buildings (11), turn left at 45° and head downhill (a marker post with a picture of wood sorrel – part of a local walks initiative – marks the spot). The path follows waymarkers, crosses a winter-only stream, then turns left to pass between the stream bed and a partly demolished wall, where once there was a stile. From here, go straight ahead down along a well-used path. At the foot of the hill, go through a stile and over Harrop Brook by means of the rebuilt packhorse bridge (12), one of the many attractive features of the Gritstone Trail.

Continue over the top of the hill and follow waymarkers and stiles to a large stone-built private house, previously The Cheshire Hunt pub. Leave the field by the stile to the left of the house (13), turn right along the track for a short distance, then left at a gate opposite the front door of the house. Walk across a meadow that's a delight in springtime. Go only as far as the first stile, which you cross and descend steps, then turn left and walk along the road.

Fork right and continue downhill to the Poachers Arms (14), where you turn left and walk along Mill Lane, past the bowling green to a minor road. You should recognise where you are now – turn right and head back to Church Street. Temptingly, you pass 'The Crown' and, depending on where you parked, 'The Church House Inn'. So many choices ...

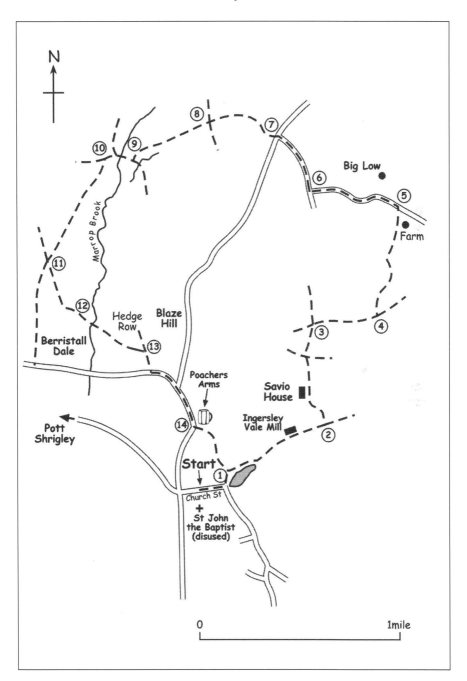

N

⑧
⑨
⑩
⑦
Big Low ●
⑥
⑤
Marrop Brook
Farm ●
⑪
⑫
Hedge Row
Blaze Hill
④
③
Berristall Dale
⑬
Poachers Arms
Savio House
Ingersley Vale Mill
②
⑭
Pott Shrigley
Start
①
Church St
✝
St John the Baptist (disused)

0   1mile

Walk: B4
The Saddle of Kerridge

Starting Point: Pool Bank car park, Palmerston Street, opposite the Spinners Arms SJ938778.

How to get there: the car park is part-way up the hill from the traffic lights below the aqueduct

Map: OS Explorer 268 – Wilmslow, Macclesfield & Congleton

Length: 3½ miles

Grade: Moderate

Duration: An hour and a half

This is an ideal evening stroll and it also introduces you to Bollington, with a bird's eye view of the town, a glimpse of the town's quarrying history and the famous White Nancy monument (see page 49) that's visible for miles around, so it's worth doing this walk just to satisfy your curiosity. Mostly, Nancy is a target for untalented graffiti daubers, but occasionally she's repainted or decorated for Christmas.

The starting point has been changed in this edition, making the walk slightly longer but avoiding the problem of parking in Chancery Lane. So, having parked the car, leave Pool Bank car park, turn left and then right into High Street. This takes you past a well-laid-out square of houses and then uphill to the end of the road, where it joins Chancery Lane (1). Turn left to steps and a footpath sign on your right, at the end of the terrace.

White Nancy is clearly visible from here and the path is easy to follow – go through the gate, along a paved stretch, through two stiles and straight uphill to the monument. The second section is up a rustic ('rough') stone track – a nice idea, badly executed. Despite this minor gripe, the view from the top (2) is stunning – with Bollington spread out like a map below you.

Follow the wall along the ridge, passing above a quarry on the right and, further away, the Hurdsfield industrial complex and of Macclesfield on the right, and of the village of Rainow on the left. Where the ridge wall meets a wall coming up from the right, with a mosaic hare

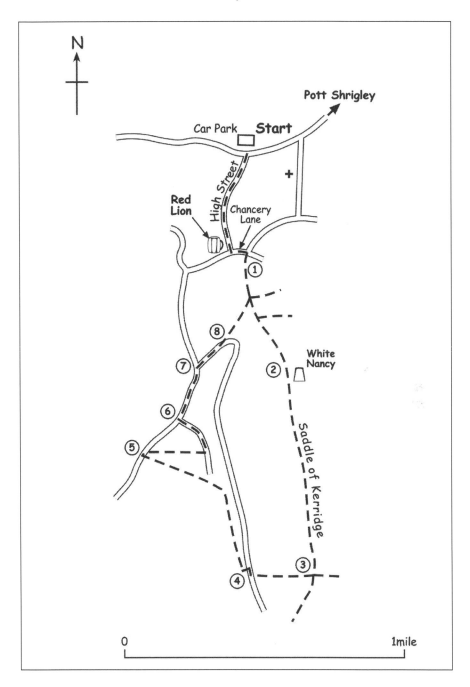

Bollington from White Nancy

at the wall corner (3), turn right and head downhill on the unsigned track. The hare is on the route of one of Bollington's excellent heritage trails – you can buy copies in the village.

Ignore a stile on the left, but continue all the way down to a concrete lane, which you follow to a road. Cross the road and almost immediately pass to the left of the entrance gates to Endon House (4). Follow the track, being careful to keep to the left of the houses, and continue to another road. Turn right here, then right again (5) at a stile and a footpath sign just past the buildings. Follow the line of the old paved mill workers' path across the field and continue alongside a wall.

Turn left at a footpath sign where the right of way meets a cobbled area and walk downhill (Adelphi Mill ahead) to the main road (6). Turn right here and, 200m later, right again into Redway, by the Bull's Head (7). At a sharp bend (8), where the Redway Tavern stood until 2003, take the footpath that forks to the left and go straight ahead between three upright stones. Follow a paved track and turn left at the next stile, walk down the steps and join the pavement at Cow Lane. Here, turn left and then right (at the Red Lion) to retrace your route down High Street.

GAWSWORTH, WINCLE & CONGLETON

These two areas are combined because of their proximity. The scenery and terrain are, however, quite different.

Gawsworth's main claim to fame is the Old Hall, dating from the late 15th century. The present owners are Mr & Mrs Timothy Richards but it has belonged to a succession of families, including the Fittons (1662 to 1702). Mary Fitton is said to be the 'Dark Lady' of Shakespeare's sonnets, and the Shakespearean connection continues today with a summer season of outdoor plays. And if you don't like Shakespeare, you can choose from Gilbert and Sullivan, jazz, brass bands, opera and modern plays. The hall is generally open from Easter to October, but not every day of the week – so you are advised to phone (01260 223456) in advance or to look at the website (www.gawsworthhall.com) for full details. Of some interest to walkers are the tea rooms – opening hours as for the hall so plan your visit accordingly.

Evening Shakespearean performance in the grounds of the Old Hall

The Georgian-style New Hall contrasts with the black-and-white architecture of the Old Hall. It is particularly impressive from the drive between the two halls, as you walk past the statues and ornamental fish ponds. The New Hall achieved some notoriety when its original owner, Lord Mohun, lost his life in one of the last duels fought in England. The stewards at the duel were accused of being accomplices to murder.

The odd-shaped house between the two halls is known as The Watch Tower. One possible reason for its existence was to overlook the surrounding lands and forest, though some believe that its thick walls might suggest that it was also used as some sort of prison.

Whereas Gawsworth lies mainly in flat farmland, Wincle stands amid the hills above the Dane valley. Although Wincle does not share Gawsworth's architectural claims to fame, it is just as popular – though its visitors tend to wear hiking boots rather than high-heeled shoes. Useful places to know about are The Ship Inn and the nearby trout farm – though I've always been squeamish when choosing trout then seeing them despatched with a stick called, believe it or not, a 'priest'.

Congleton is just on the edge of our Cheshire walks, being near the Staffordshire border. For walkers, its main claim to fame is The Cloud, a hilly outcrop with identifiable remains of Bronze Age settlements. Around the area there are many other sites of interest, including the Bridestones Neolithic burial chamber. Congleton has an active Ramblers' Association, with members dividing their time between Cheshire and Staffordshire.

The Walks

Of all the areas covered in this book, these must rank as favourites. The area around Wincle, in particular, is just hilly enough to be stimulating, but without losing its greenness, as do some of the wilder parts of the Peak District. A section of the Gritstone Trail passes through Wincle and that, of course, is included. Most walkers from Wincle cross the Dane into Derbyshire, but the walk suggested here is a purely Cheshire affair.

Walk: GWC1
Gawsworth and North Rode

Starting Point: Road alongside St James's Church, Gawsworth SJ890698. Parking at a precise spot can be a problem around here – it is justifiably popular. Be sure not to park in the Hall car park – this is for the use of Hall patrons only.

How to get there: Gawsworth is signposted from the A636 Macclesfield/Congleton road, and from Broken Cross in Macclesfield.

Map: OS Explorer 268 – Wilmslow, Macclesfield & Congleton

Length: 6½ miles

Grade: Easy

Duration: Three hours

The scenery around here is quintessentially English, and you can easily fit this walk into a summer evening. There is a stretch of road to be walked, but it's normally quiet. While walking the route on a September day, the weather was glorious after a record-breaking wet summer. Perhaps the rain was responsible for the luscious blackberries along the way!

Our walk begins at St James's Church (1).

> The pool in front of the church provided carp for the clergy, while the one near the hall doubtless supplied the nobility. If you have time, pop into the church, which dates back over 500 years; you can see the splendid monuments and effigies of the Fitton family – including that of Mary Fitton, mentioned in the introduction to this section.

St James's Church, Gawsworth, with fish pond

Leave the church behind, on your left, and walk down the lane. Turn left and up some steps at the 'North Rode' signpost, over a stile and into a field, after which the footpath continues straight ahead. The hill ahead is Bosley Cloud – a very recognisable landmark visited on walk GWC3. More to your left, you'll see the Sutton Common radio mast, a prominent feature on the Gritstone Trail.

After crossing the third of three more stiles, against a holly hedge, fork left to a large fishing lake. When, in 2004, I first saw this lake – and another one beyond – I reached for my OS Explorer map and found that the right of way is shown running through both lakes! Luckily, an action replay of my seven-year campaign to reclaim a right of way, as described in walk W5, will not be necessary as the necessary official diversions have been made – perhaps somebody should tell the OS! So – walk past the first lake and, just a few yards past the start of the second one, bear right to a stile. Cross this and follow waymarks and the hedgeline to the next stile. The path now continues virtually straight ahead through a series of stiles to the road (2), which you cross. Carry on down Pexall Road, turn left at the first footpath sign on the left (3) and continue straight ahead to Manor Farm. The path is to the right of the main farm buildings, and crosses a stile just to the left of a white-painted brick barn (the building on the extreme right).

Continue straight ahead from here along the drive, ignoring the left turn. At the end of the drive, go over a cattle grid and face a cottage (4). You are now in North Rode, but before continuing with the walk, here is a small diversion: turn right and continue to a T-junction with Daintry Hall (village hall and nursery) on the right – built in memory of the last squire of North Rode. More interesting is St Michael's church, on the left – an absolute gem.

Though Victorian (built in 1845) it looks substantially older – see photograph on next page. The square tower is crowned with a circular turret; inside, there is some excellent stained glass, with windows in memory of squires, clergy and other local folk. There is a superb carved oak screen and choir stalls, and a framed hymn sheet from the consecration of the church in 1846. And the greatest surprise is that it's open for visitors!

From here, retrace your steps along the lane and then a farm drive, to pass the buildings of Yew Tree Farm (also a B&B) on the right. Cross a stile into a field and continue alongside a fence on your right. Leave the field by the next stile, turn right and follow the tarmac drive of North

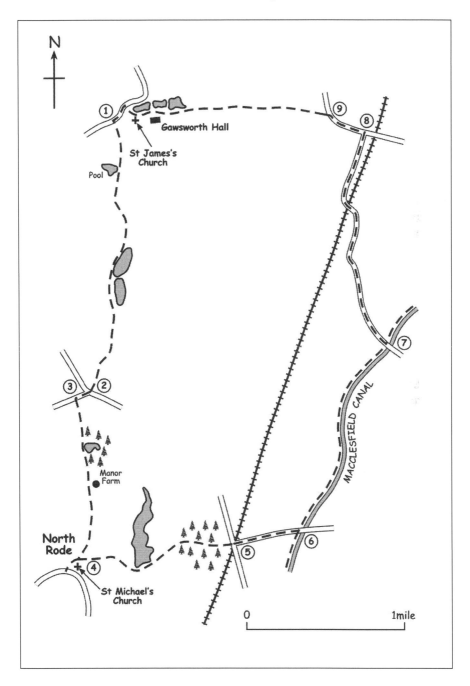

The unusual church at North Rode, complete with both tower and turret

Rode manor, passing a large lake *en route*. Lakes are popular around here. At the end of the drive, cross over the railway bridge (5) and follow the road ahead to the canal bridge, at the top of Bosley Locks. Turn left (6), passing the colourful moored boats and follow the towpath of the Macclesfield Canal for a mile or so to bridge number 51, where you turn left (7) to join a country road.

For the next mile or so, follow the road (not the farm track) to a T-junction, where you turn left past Railway Cottage (8) to Gawsworth (9). Just after a farm on your left, fork left along a signposted track.

Soon you have a great view of the Lovell radio telescope at Jodrell Bank: if it's other than flat, it's hard at work – perhaps listening out for a galactic hitch-hiker.

Continue through a series of kissing gates and stiles, back to Gawsworth. This latter part of the walk takes you past picturesque cottages and yet another fishing lake in front of the New Hall. If the Old Hall is open (see opening times on noticeboard or go to www.gawsworthhall.com for full details), change your hiking boots and soak up some local history – and/or visit the tea rooms.

Walk: GWC2

Wincle to Sutton Common, along the Gritstone Trail

Starting Point: Roadside below The Ship Inn, Wincle SJ962653

How to get there: A523 from Macclesfield then left on the A54 at Bosley crossroads and follow signs to Wincle. Park on a wide part of the road, even if it means parking much further down the hill.

Map: OS Explorer 268 – Wilmslow, Macclesfield & Congleton

Length: 9½ miles

Grade: Moderate/strenuous

Duration: Five hours

The Gritstone Trail is a famous cross-country walk which originally ran from Lyme Park to Rushton Spencer – a distance of about 20 miles. It has been extended to a total of 35 miles by adding the former Mow Cop Trail and details are available at www.cheshire.gov.uk/countryside/walking. Mere mortals can no longer complete the trail in a day, but if you fancy a circular walk that includes just part of it, here's your chance.

Walk uphill from The Ship and after 50m climb a flight of stone steps on your left (1). Bear right across the field to the opposite stile, to the right of the buildings – but beware of natural hazards, such as the close encounter that I had here:

I was sitting on top of the stile, checking the route, when I heard some huffing and puffing immediately behind me. I looked over my shoulder to find a large black bull (with ring through nose) sniffing my posterior. I thought that he just seemed inquisitive, though a trainee vet told me that they sniff to establish if a heifer is in heat! I was later advised that it must have been my lucky day, as that particular bull was "a dangerous b****r".

So – go across a drive, over a stile and follow the stone wall on your left. At the end of this wall, cross the stile and head uphill through the wood, then over another stile. Bear right across a field and cross a stile onto a lane.

Turn left and follow the lane towards, but not past, Wincle Grange Farm (2).

> The ecclesiastical style of the buildings is worth noting, as the farm was used by a Cistercian order of monks as a distribution centre for wool – a hugely profitable trade in the 14th to 15th centuries. The monks were remarkably worldly-wise and good businessmen too, with considerable properties often many miles from head office.

As you approach the farm, ignore the first stile to the left of a gateway. Instead, bear left *through* the gateway and follow a path with a prefabricated barn on your left and the farm buildings on your right. Go through three (not very rambler-friendly) steel gates and cross a stile, with waymark. Slant downhill, aiming just to the left of the junction of a fence and an overgrown hedge. Continue straight ahead from here, into the corner of the field, then follow the hedge (on your right) downhill.

Cross the stile level with a farm – Nettlebeds – on your right (3), turn right over a stile by a gate, then left and downhill. The high ridge ahead of you is Wincle Minn, on the route to Croker Hill.

Head downhill through a steel gate in fencing and continue from here down the slope, following the general line of power cables. At the bottom of the hill, you will find a fence running alongside a stream and, at the extreme left-hand corner of this fence, a smaller stream joins the main one. Cross the footbridge here and continue to follow the line of the power cables steeply uphill. As the terrain levels out, the path leaves the line of cables on the left and continues with a wood on the right, a farm straight ahead in the distance and a new house, further to the right.

Follow the path to the extreme end of another wood on your left. Pass a gate at this point and follow the grassy track towards Hawkslee Farm (4). The right of way goes straight ahead, across the end of the farm garden and uphill to a stile. Cross this and turn right to follow the Gritstone Trail (a surfaced track along this stretch) for a mile or so, with stunning views across to the left on a clear day.

> With luck, the whole of the Cheshire Plain can be seen, from Jodrell Bank to Manchester Airport and as far as Fidlers Ferry power station on the coast.

As the track climbs still further, a flat-topped Shutlingsloe can be admired but eventually you finish climbing and the track curves down to the main road (5) – be sure to follow the track and don't be tempted to take a short cut!

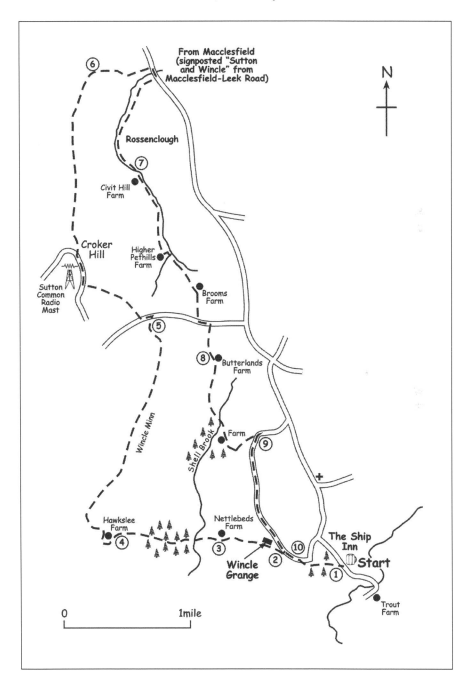

Turn left at the road and follow it for 100m to a footpath sign on your right. Turn right here and head uphill towards the Sutton Common (Croker Hill) telecommunications mast – the route is obvious and well waymarked. It joins a track through a stile to the right of a farm building. Turn right and follow the track past the radio mast.

After about 200m, at a major junction, leave the main track and fork right along a well-used but often boggy route. You are still on the Gritstone Trail and the path lies straight ahead – just follow the waymarks with the familiar Gritstone symbol all the way to the road. The only potential problem arises after a long downhill stretch with a wall on your right. Where the path levels out, cross a stile on the right (6) and head downhill, but moving away from the wall (on your left) and onto a broad green track to the right of a reedy mini-ravine. Pass through or above an area of gorse, then left of a small wood to an elaborate wall stile with a welcoming Gritstone marker. Continue ahead to a concessionary path around Foxbank Farm – there is a right of way through the property, but it's no shorter and there are no views, so there's not much point in asserting your rights on this occasion!

Go down to the road and turn right, then almost immediately right again along a crumbling tarmac lane. Just before the first building on the left, Kinderfields Farm, there is a stile which offers a high level alternative – for those who want it – through Lower Pethills. However, my preferred route passes Kinderfields and, after half a mile, also passes Rossenclough (marked on the map as Redwood Farm) on your left.

In 300m, cross a cattle grid at the entrance to Civit Hills (also called Civit Hall) Farm (7). After about 50m, after a cattle grid, fork left through a gate but keep to the higher track, away from the swamp below. You soon pass through a second gate with a pool on your left. From here, descend to (but not across) the stream and turn right, heading upstream. Cross a small tributary coming in from the right and soon you pass the Lower Pethills property over to your left.

The path heads uphill to a gate (waymark) and straight to Higher Pethills. Pass between the main buildings, turn left, then – shortly before a cattle grid – turn right at a footpath/bridleway sign. The path continues towards the next buildings – the considerably developed 'Broome Farm', now surrounded by a ranch-stile stockade fence. There are currently no waymarks to guide you but, at the fence, turn right and continue to a gate. Turn left through this and exit through the larger gate opposite – where there is a waymark. Turn right onto the drive and head for the road,

Autumn sunlight in Greasley Hollow

where you turn left – but glance over your shoulder and you'll see the Croker Hill tower again. Very soon, turn right onto a public footpath just before the entrance to Butterlands Farm (8).

Our route originally proceeded due south and through the farm. However, in late 2010, there was a major official diversion, which has been signposted. In brief: the public path through Butterlands has been stopped up and a diversion takes you around and roughly parallel to the original route before re-joining it down Nabbs Hill.

In a bit more detail: having turned right at grid reference SJ946674 on the new right-of-way (FP3A), continue south-west for 300m to a kissing gate (SJ944672). From here, turn left and walk in a south-south-easterly direction for a further 300m to a junction of paths (SJ945670), then turn left again to head east for about 50m to a second kissing gate (SJ946670). Turn right (south-south-west), soon passing through yet another kissing gate on the diverted public path PF4 before joining the original FP4 at SJ947668 to start heading downhill, down Nabbs Hill.

You are soon walking along a very obviously broad green track down to the ridge of the hill, with a steep ravine on your right. Continue down the hill, to an enormous kissing gate and stile.

You are now descending into the appropriately-named Greasley Hollow. The banks are steep, muddy and often slippery here. In springtime, however, there are lovely displays of bluebells and the autumn colours are a treat – but watch your step!

Having negotiated the descent, cross a footbridge to a path on the opposite bank and head uphill at a 45-degree angle to the stream, along a well-used path. Cross a stile and head to the right, keeping the fence on your right. Pass Lower Greasley – a farm surrounded by assorted scrap metal, that has seen better days. Veer slightly right and turn left over a stile, then follow the farm track. Where the track joins a lane (9), turn right and head back to Wincle Grange.

Pass the farm buildings, noting yet more of its ecclesiastical features, then a pool on your right and continue along the lane, downhill. After about 150m, cross a stone stile on your right (10). Enter the field and head for the wood, your path making an angle of 45° with the wall on your left. Cross the next stile and head through the wood, rejoining the original path that soon crosses the farm drive and takes you back to your starting point. (I spotted my friendly bull again but skirted the edge of the field – just in case.)

Walk: GWC3

Timbersbrook, Bosley Cloud, Rushton Spencer, and The Bridestones

Starting Point: Timbersbrook Picnic Site SJ895627

How to get there: from Macclesfield, head south on the A523 and cross the A54. After a further 1½ miles turn right on minor road that heads towards the Cloud and head directly to Timbersbrook; turn right in the village centre and the car park is on the right.

Map: OS Explorer 268 – Wilmslow, Macclesfield & Congleton

Length: 7½ miles

Grade: Easy/Moderate

Duration: Three and a half hours

This 'East Cheshire' walk is a bit of a cheat: it starts in Cheshire, but much of it is in Staffordshire! The problem I had was that it seemed a good idea to include a walk up The Cloud but – having got there – where to go? A glance at the map shows that the only logical route is east, towards Rushton Spencer and Staffordshire – and none the worse for that. On the return journey, a neolithic burial chamber is included to add a spot of culture.

Leave the car at Timbersbrook Picnic Site (1) – once the centre of a thriving little hamlet based on a dyeing and bleaching works (see letterhead, below) that used the Timbers Brook for motive power. Leave the car park through a gate to a picnic site then go up some steps and turn left onto a road (Tunstall Road). After about 250m turn right (2) at a

The Silver Springs works, 1925, as seen on the picnic site display board

'Gritstone Trail' sign and climb steeply uphill on a stepped trail. At a wide track (Gosberryhole Lane) turn right and continue all the way to a National Trust sign for 'The Cloud'.

Walk along the track indicated by this sign until you reach an oak wood with a choice of routes (3). I suggest that you fork left on the track that contours around the wood, so that you can admire the open views on your left as you walk up to the trig point, which is *just* in Staffordshire. From here, carry on in the direction you've been walking, heading downhill along a track which ends in an over-civilised flight of concrete steps. At the foot of these, turn left and go down a track to the road.

At the road, turn left (4), walk downhill and then turn right (footpath sign for The Staffordshire Way and The Gritstone Trail) and cross a stile with the 'knot' sign for The Staffordshire Way. Keep a wall, then a fence, on your right along a well-used path that is waymarked with both Staffordshire Way and Gritstone Trail markers until, after two stiles, you notice that the route forks left, into a wood. There is a waymark in this direction for The Staffordshire Way. (**Note:** this used to be a concessionary route but, by the time you read this book, is almost certain to be the right of way.)

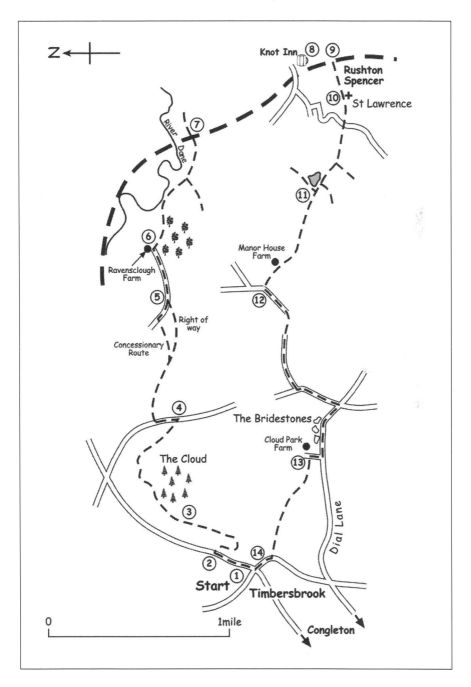

Follow the waymark through the wood and go downhill to a lane; turn right and continue for about 300m along the lane to a group of agricultural buildings on your right.

Continue to Ravensclough Farm (6). Turn right before the farm and aim for the edge of the wood. The path runs through the wood and then crosses a stream. From here, cross a meadow, with a nice view of the River Dane on the left. Keep the field boundary on your left and eventually, as you approach the far left corner of the field, you will see a railway bridge. Head towards this and continue to a stile in the corner, cross another stream and turn right (over a stile) onto the route of the dismantled railway track (7) to Rushton Spencer. The railway was the Churnet Valley branch of the North Staffordshire Railway.

After about a mile you reach the Knot Inn at Rushton Spencer (8) – a good place to wine and dine at the right time. Pass between the Knot and the old station house (dated 1841) on the right. Walk along the track-bed and under a large, stone arch bridge (9). Shortly after, go left up some steps, then over a stile and turn left – which means that you have actually turned right at the bridge! From here, follow a path to the church of St Lawrence (10).

> This intriguing building has a small, wooden tower and gravestones dating back to 1610. It is set in a lonely, beautiful stretch of countryside but is – regrettably – usually locked; a sign of the times.

Go through the churchyard to a track, crossing over a minor road to a stile. From this point, there is a disagreement with the OS map. If you attempt to follow the theoretical right of way, you will end up on the wrong side of a barbed wire fence and one of my readers, Robin Salmon, suggests these instructions: "On the far side of the field, almost straight ahead, are two very similar trees. The stile is to the left of the left tree. Once across, turn about 30° to the right and head over a slight rise to a pond (11), surrounded by some trees. The top of a distant electricity pylon is a good aiming point. Skirt round the right-hand side of the pond and cross the stile." I agree.

Head uphill with the hedge on your left. The path then takes you past what was Ditchway Farm (now 'Manor House') on your right, over a stile and along a farm drive to the road, where you turn left (12).

From here, there's some unavoidable road walking – so take care. Follow this minor road, keeping left at the first junction, with some farm buildings. Continue for about half a mile to another T-junction where you turn left again, in the indicated direction to 'Biddulph and Congleton'. After about 300m, turn right on a minor road (from grid reference 910621 to 909621) to join the road to Congleton, Dial Lane. Turn right here and, after about 200m, pass the entrance to the house called "The Bridestones". Turn right up a farm drive and, just before the farmyard, turn left to view the site of The Bridestones Neolithic burial chamber.

Its discovery was almost accidental – but the most surprising aspect was its size: approximately 10m wide by 100m long, though only a small part can now be visited. There were three burial chambers, but two of them were used for building materials in the 18th century. If you look around the immediate vicinity, you'll see that rocks from the burial chamber were used to construct garden walls until the archaeological significance of the site was recognised. There are many other burial chambers around here (such as the impressive mound at Cleulow Cross, above Wincle) – so look with interest at any large hump in the ground, but don't start excavating; you would not only be a vandal, but also in clear breach of the law.

From The Bridestones, go back to the road (Dial Lane), turn right in the direction of Congleton and take the first turn right down a tarmac lane (13) towards Cloud Park Farm. After about 50m, turn left across the stone wall (public footpath sign). After a couple of hundred metres,

The Bridestones

continue ahead and alongside a wooded area on your right, with a fine view of Jodrell Bank. (**Note to footpath purists:** the OS map indicates that this is where the right of way finishes. However, I have established with reasonable certainty that this was an oversight by the relevant authorities and I am confident that you are within your rights to follow these instructions. You also avoid some additional road walking.)

So, keep the field boundary (this being the County boundary) on your right and carry on – after a similar distance there used to be a stile, but no longer. Continue for a further quarter of a mile towards another wooded area coming in from the left. Where the two meet, there is a stile tucked away in the corner, down towards a dip, where you cross the stream – and return to Cheshire. From here, head to a stile in the wall (14). Turn right and follow the road – passing the mill pool for the Timbersbrook works – to a crossroads, where you go straight across in the Congleton direction along Weathercock Lane, and back to the car park.

KETTLESHULME & RAINOW

These are hill-country villages, well known to walking connoisseurs – though on many Saturday afternoons, I have walked for miles around here and never seen a soul. Sheep outnumber humans, but sensitive housing development has seen an influx of people preferring to live in the country than suburbia. Rainow, being nearer to Macclesfield, is the larger of the two and has quite a lively community, and its own website www.rainowvillage.co.uk. There's less to say about Kettleshulme but it does have a tradition of entertaining road signs:

Renowned for its road signs: the one on the right once also said '... or a sheep'

Like many of the surrounding towns and villages, these two reached their peak in the late 19th and early 20th centuries. At one time, Rainow alone had 13 mills and 9 public houses. The mills were of various types – silk, cotton and fustian – even a candlewick mill at Lumb Hole, Rainow, on the banks of Todd Brook. A large proportion of the workforce was home-based, weaving at small looms in the cottages. The materials for this cottage industry came from nearby Macclesfield or Bollington, thus explaining the numerous paved footpaths that cross the open countryside.

Apart from weaving, another major industry was engineering – both in its own right and as a service to local farmers. Surprisingly, the engineering was of the heavy variety, producing steam rollers, steam hammers and the like. A local yarn is told of John Mellor, a Rainow engineer who manufactured steam rollers. One of his early models became stuck in a muddy Rainow field, much to the delight of local farmers who offered to remove it with their 'more dependable' horses. Mr Mellor refused, insisted that he would drive his roller out of the mud – and he did, thus helping to assure the progress of engineering and the demise of horses as working farm animals.

Both weaving and engineering declined in these relatively remote villages as Macclesfield and Stockport increased in importance. There are no surviving mills – the last one was the Swan Vale in Kettleshulme and this closed in 1979. Quarrying, however, continued until relatively recently, up to 1000 men being employed in the industry at one time. Nowadays, hill farming is the order of the day, though few of the farms appear to be very prosperous. Perhaps the largest local undertaking is Lamaload reservoir: the North West Water Board owns large tracts of land locally, but its employees are few in number – water has a habit of looking after itself.

The Walks

This is a stimulating area for walkers. The scenery is superb, including small lowland farms, tumbling streams and rugged hills. The most impressive stretch of hill walking is along the Tors (Shining Tor, Cat's Tor along to Pym Chair) which separate Cheshire from Derbyshire. The entire area, including the Water Board land, is criss-crossed by a superb network of paths, and I am pleased to report that the provision of stiles, signs and waymarks has improved immensely since the first edition of this book.

Walk: KR1
Lamaload, The Tors and Pym Chair

Starting Point: Car Park, east of Lamaload reservoir SJ976753. If the car park entrance is locked, use the lay-by which is uphill, about 150m NE of the car park entrance.

How to get there: From the B5470 Macclesfield-Whaley Bridge Road, take either of the minor roads (Pike Road or Smith Lane) that head east. These roads converge and pass Blue Boar Farm before heading downhill to a road junction where you keep right and continue for a few hundred metres to the car park.

Map: OS Explorer OL 24 – The Peak District, White Peak Area

Length: 7 miles

Grade: Moderate/strenuous

Duration: Three and a half hours

This magnificent walk is reminiscent of some of the finest Welsh hill walking – a rare compliment as far as I am concerned. Although the hills are steep, the paths are easy to find, giving you plenty of time to admire the views.

Access to the car park is usually from the junction with the A5002 (see map) and is signposted to the Goyt Valley. On your way down the road, look out for the small stone memorial describing the dastardly deed of over 200 years ago when John Turner was found dead in the snow in suspicious circumstances. It's tricky to park your car here, but one side of the stone is shown alongside; the reverse reads, ominously:

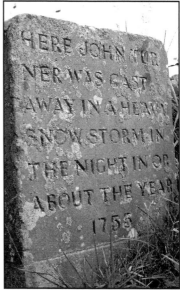

> The print of a woman's shoe
> Was found by his side
> Where he lay dead

So, if you spot a suspicious-looking stranger, hurry on your way. Otherwise, from the car park, go back to the road and turn right. Turn left at the bridge (1), along a grassy track signposted to 'Burbage and Shining Tor'. The path goes steeply uphill, alongside a stream. As the stream runs slightly to the right, continue straight ahead to a stile. From here, follow the track and head for a large gap, roughly mid-way along a stone wall on the skyline.

At the wall (2), fork right and converge on the wall to your right. Follow the wall. Some fine views open out ahead of you, including Shutlingsloe from about point (3) on the map, where the path levels out. The Sutton Common tower is also clearly visible, slightly to your right.

For the final stretch, the route bends left before crossing another path (4) and heading straight up the steep hill towards Shining Tor (5). At the top of the ridge, visit the triangulation point by turning right and following the track to a stile on your right: the trig point is actually on private land, but concessionary access is provided.

Having been to the highest point in Cheshire, retrace your steps and head north along the broad – almost straight – track all the way to Cat's Tor and Pym Chair (6). If you have chosen to do this walk at any time but high summer, you'll quickly discover what a soggy place this can be, and why many seasoned walkers can be seen in wellies around here!

At the end of the ridge, almost facing Pym Chair car park, turn left to head downhill and westwards until the road levels out just after Pymchair Farm (7). To avoid a further stretch of road walking, turn right at a footpath sign and go over two stiles towards the renovated Green Stack Farm. Turn left along the stony drive and pass a very derelict barn on your right. The right of way is shown leaving the drive and soon rejoining it, so you might as well stay on the drive until you see Jenkin Chapel ahead, to the right of a clump of trees. Where the drive crosses the remains of a dry-stone wall, fork right towards the chapel, cross two fields, cross a stile and turn right to rejoin the road and reach Jenkin Chapel (8). Follow the path, signposted to Rainow, which is opposite to the chapel. Head directly away from the chapel, over the hill and towards a barn at the foot of the hill.

Cross a stile in the stone wall, some 50m before the corner in the wall. Then, cross the footbridge (9). Turn right in front of the barn (10) – go over the stile in the wall – turn left after going through an opening in the wire fence and walk uphill, following a wall at first, then the remains of a hedge. Cross a stile and head slightly to the right over a stile into a wood (11). Follow the obvious path to a stile in the top-right-hand corner of the wood.

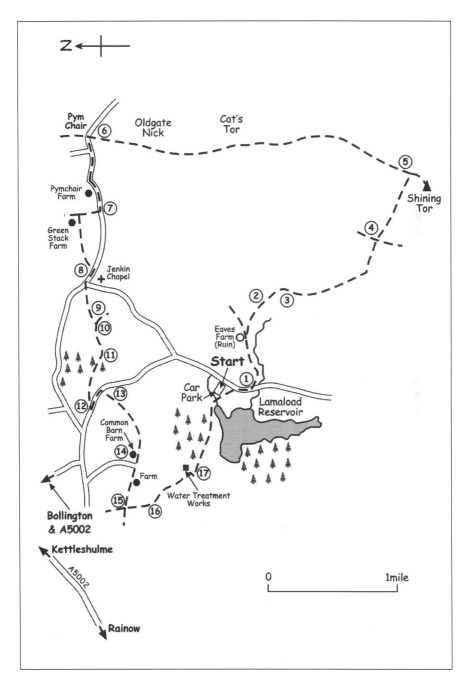

Jenkin Chapel

Follow the path alongside a wall, go over a stile and cross the field to a stile in a fence. Continue straight ahead to a stile in the wall at the road (12). Turn left and then right, at a gate (13), after about 100m. Walk along the track and through the gate into a farmyard. Fork right over a stile and pass behind the farmhouse. Lamaload is now in sight, on your left.

From this farmhouse, follow the track to a short, tumbledown wall which you keep on your left – the next stile is in the corner of the wall facing you. Cross the stile and go straight ahead to a stile with a footpath signpost. Go over this stile and follow the path towards the next farm – Common Barn (14) – keeping the wall on your right. Go over another stile and into the farmyard.

Cross the farmyard, following the waymarks through metal gates to a stile into a field. Follow the wall on your right as far as the next stile (15), where you turn left. Join the farm track coming in from the right (16) and head downhill with the house on your right. A well-used path takes you towards the water treatment works.

Turn right at the corner of the garden of one of the houses (17), and then after a few yards turn left at a footpath sign to head uphill. Pass through a prominent gap in the wall near the top of the hill. Head to the right from here and join a track with the wall on your right, all the way back to the car park.

Walk: KR2

A Walk around Lamaload

Starting Point: Car Park, east of Lamaload Reservoir SJ976753. If the entrance is locked, use the lay-by, about 150m NE and uphill from the car park entrance.

How to get there: From the B5470 Macclesfield-Whaley Bridge Road, take either of the minor roads (Pike Road or Smith Lane) that head east. These roads converge and pass Blue Boar Farm before heading downhill to a road junction where you keep right and continue for a few hundred metres to the car park.

Map: OS Explorer OL 24 – The Peak District, White Peak Area

Length: 5 miles

Grade: Moderate/strenuous

Duration: Two and a half hours

This takes you through countryside that is isolated and beautiful – yet so accessible for a motorist lucky enough to own a pair of boots. Depending on how energetic you feel, you may wish to complete just this walk or to link up with Walk KR3 which takes you over to Macclesfield Forest.

Walk from the car park towards the reservoir, and to the right of the toilet block which is in a large stone building. Turn right just before the building and continue for about 30m, joining a track that leads to a stile (1). Cross this and continue on a path over the hill and through a large gap in the wall towards the water treatment buildings (2) below the dam.

Follow the path down the hill, and towards the buildings. At the foot of the hill, turn left, and cross a stream. Walk along a track, between a pair of stone walls. At a gate, keep right along a paved path, then turn left at the access road and walk along this for about one mile, passing firstly Snipe House Farm (3) and then Higherlane Farm (4).

The road now dips (5) – as it rises again, Bollington and White Nancy are visible straight ahead. 50m after the second building on your left after Higherlane Farm, and just before a cattle grid, cross a stone stile set into the wall. There is (or was) a permissive path, which you can use if you feel inclined. But to use the right of way (which scarcely intrudes on anyone's privacy) just head diagonally to your left (6), crossing the stile set in the stone wall near the back gate of the smartened-up house on your left.

The classic view of Lamaload

Carry on in the same direction, uphill, and cross the next stile in the wall facing you. Continue uphill, with the wall on your immediate right. Just before the remains of a wall jutting out to the left, cross the stile on your right. Turn left and again head uphill, with the wall initially on your immediate left and Newbuildings Farm further to your left. As the wall turns away leftwards, carry on in the same direction that you were heading and cross a stone step-stile by a gate (7).

Turn right here, walking along the farm track. Ignore the signpost for the Gritstone Trail, and continue along the track (with a good view across to Jodrell Bank in clear weather) until you reach a group of buildings based on Hordern Farm. Continue past all these and through a gate (8). Walk along a well-used track, initially with a wall on your left, above the small valley of Gulshaw Hollow. Continue alongside the remains of a dry-stone wall to a stile across a stream (9).

Go uphill about 100m and turn left along a concrete track towards what I originally described as "a near-derelict farmhouse".

Not any more! It's now a superb modern home, and the right of way still runs through the grounds. Begin in a novel way by pressing '2' and then '#' on a keypad and the gate slides open just far enough, and long enough, for a walker to pass through. I'd never seen anything like this before!

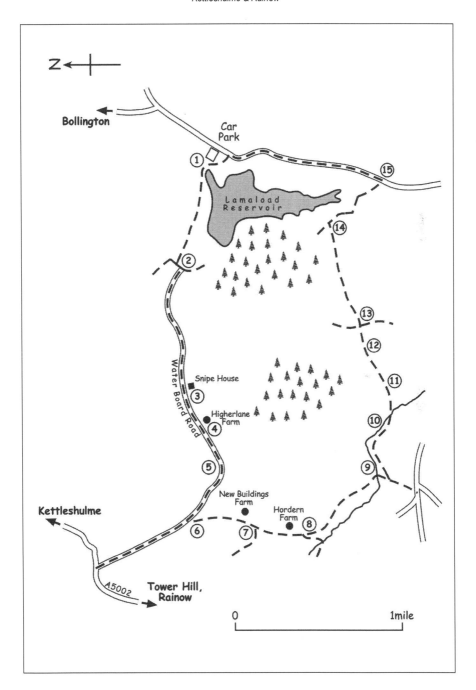

Continue on the driveway, bear right and pass the house on your left then proceed to a stile. Cross this, then follow the track over a stream and pass a barn on your left (10). From here, head left with the wall on your left. After the wall has bent to the right, you will see a stone stile. Cross this (or one of the many gaps) and continue in the same direction – heading over the hill using the wall on the skyline (11) as your marker. From here, carry straight on to another stile set in a wall, and likewise to the next one.

After crossing the hill, the next stile is a wooden one in the top-right-hand corner of the field (12). Cross this and head along a path making an approximately 45° angle with the stream. This takes you off again in roughly the same direction of travel as before, towards a line of power cables.

Cross the farm drive (13) and enter the next field across a stile near a gateway. Continue straight ahead, with the wall on your right. Cross a stile and footbridge and carry on, soon with a wall on your right. After about 200m, do a wiggle through a gateway to put the wall on your left (don't follow the direction of the waymark, which will take you much too far to the right). In the corner of the field, cross a stile and head towards the left of a conifer plantation; Lamaload can be seen on your left.

Carry on downhill to the abandoned building and turn right at the track (14). After a few minutes, cross a stile into the wood – the stile is marked as leading to a path and has a "Danger, Deep Water" sign nearby. Follow this concessionary path through the wood and up to the road (15) where you turn left and head back to the car park.

Walk: KR3

Tegg's Nose, Langley and Macclesfield Forest

Starting Point: Car Park (charge, but toilets are free), Tegg's Nose Country Park SJ950733.

How to get there: From Macclesfield take the A537 in the direction of Buxton and, after about a mile, fork right on Buxton Old Road. Tegg's Nose is on the right after just over a mile.

Map: OS Explorer OL 24 – The Peak District, White Peak Area

Length: 6 miles

Grade: Moderate/strenuous

Duration: Three hours

Some years ago, while at Tegg's Nose, a hot-air balloon was drifting lazily across the distant hills and there was not a cloud in the sky. It's not always like that – many more years ago we brought our daughters here with their sledges and the snow was up to our knees, with barely a smattering down the hill in Macclesfield. But, whatever the weather, a good place to start this walk is at the collection of five viewfinders at one side of the car-park, looking south-east across Macclesfield Forest and towards Shutlingsloe. Rather than simply identifying distant landmarks, these illustrate some of the walks that can be done from here.

Leave the viewfinders (1) and follow the bridleway (Saddlers Way) downhill. At the T-junction at the foot of the hill, turn right along a lane to a junction (2) with direction stones pointing left to Macclesfield Forest and Forest Chapel, and ahead to Clough House Farm. Take neither of these but fork right on a track signed to Langley. The path climbs slightly before dropping down again: take care not to branch off to the right – the path you want runs alongside the wall.

Cross over a stream, go uphill a short way, and follow the track which eventually leads to Teggsnose Reservoir (3), seen on your right. At the far end of this reservoir, turn left at a footpath sign and walk along the track around Bottoms Reservoir until you reach the road.

Turn left here, walk along the road and up the hill to the Leather's

Smithy pub (4). Fork left at the pub and continue uphill, passing a cottage with a sign in the garden jokingly telling us that "A lovely lady and a grumpy old man live here".

A little further uphill, there's a notice nailed to a footpath sign stating that the footpath to Topclose Farm is a cul-de-sac and there's no point in using it. Maybe it was written by the same grumpy old man. Or maybe it would be public-spirited to extend it through the farm to make a nice circular stroll for local people.

I digress – as you go over the top of the hill (about a quarter of a mile), fork left on a bridleway into Macclesfield Forest (5). The track climbs through the forest, following the bridleway and ignoring side turns.

Eventually, as the path levels out, you'll see an old stone-built building (6) at the fork of two tracks. Take the left fork, walking past the building on your immediate right. After about 100m, fork right along a minor path – there is a 'Walker Barn' signpost here.

The path emerges from the forest to meet a road, Hacked Way Lane (7). Turn left and, after a few paces, turn right across a stile to follow the boundary of the house, Ashtreetop, on your right. Cross another stile and go straight ahead, following a tumbledown dry-stone wall. The path dips to where you cross a stream and continues almost straight ahead on a zigzag route through gorse and hawthorne. Follow this steep track/path over a rise and drop to another dip and another stream. Cross this, then climb steeply (waymark) through more scrub to join the next derelict wall. Climb over a stile and pass below Warrilowhead Farm (8) and cross a stile to join the access drive.

After 100m or so, fork left off the drive at a right-hand bend towards a ladder stile. Cross this and follow waymarks to a stile to the right of a group of farm buildings, where you join a lane and turn right to the main road. Cross this busy road and pass to the right of a barn which, in turn, is to the right of what used to be the Setter Dog pub.

An odd thing happened here: as I was busily photographing the plaque commemorating the Millennium, I heard somebody calling a dog – or so I thought. In fact, an elderly lady was calling a sheep, which obediently trotted to the fence for a pat on the head and a crust of bread. Cuddling her 16-year-old cat, she told me that the sheep was a particularly sociable one, but that it had "a few other pals" that she had also befriended A touch of cupboard love for this lovely lady.

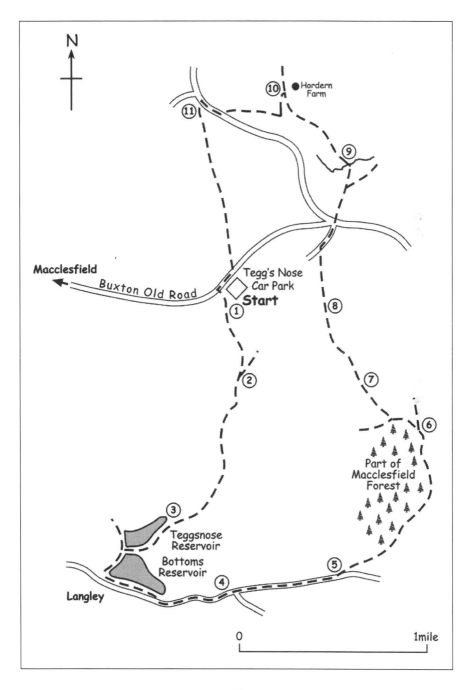

The Peak National Park boundary marker on the Macclesfield to Buxton road – just above where the Setter Dog pub was located

Walk down the concrete track and fork left onto the grass at a waymark, heading to a gate and stile. Turn left here (9) on a path above Gulshaw Hollow (also visited on Walk KR2) until just before the buildings of Hordern Farm. Go through a kissing gate and do a sharp hairpin left (10) on a tarmac drive that leads down, around and up to the main road. Turn right here and continue for 150m.

Cross the road to a collection of steps, kissing gate and footpath sign (11) – hard to miss! Follow the Gritstone Trail markers (the ones with a 'G' inside a bootprint). Continue straight ahead across this windswept landscape to the appropriately named Windyway House, turn right along the road and then left into the car park. With luck (and the right time of year) the ice-cream van will still be there.

Walk: KR4

Pym Chair, Charles Head and Windgather Rocks

Starting Point: Pym Chair, SJ996766

How to get there: Easiest to drive to Kettleshulme on the B5470 and look for the sign, near the school, pointing to Goyt Valley and Dunge Valley Gardens

Map: OS Explorer OL 24 – The Peak District, White Peak Area

Length: 7½ miles

Grade: Moderate/strenuous

Duration: Three and a half hours

It is so difficult to choose a favourite walk. And yet this one, though it includes a small amount of road-walking, must be counted as one of my personal favourites. Perhaps because of its variety – fields, streams, hills, forests and rocky outcrops – but particularly for the splendid views from Charles Head and Taxal Edge. There is some overlap with Walk KR7, but mostly in a reverse direction which is always so different!

Walk out of the car park (1), and turn left towards the T-junction. Turn right here and head towards Jenkin Chapel (2). Head downhill and westwards until the road levels out just after Pymchair Farm, then – using the same route as described in walk KR1 – i.e. turn right at a footpath sign and go over two stiles towards the renovated Green Stack Farm. Turn left along the stony drive and pass a very derelict barn on your right. The right of way is shown leaving the drive and then rejoining it, so just stay on the drive until you see Jenkin Chapel ahead, to the right of a clump of trees. Where the drive crosses the remains of a dry-stone wall, fork right towards the chapel. Cross two fields, cross a stile and turn right to rejoin the road.

Go past the chapel, straight ahead along a lane marked as a no-through road and 'No vehicles except for access'. Go down a steep hill, then up the other side – partly cobbled – until, just after passing a wood on your left, and before gates across the track, you'll see a stile on your right (3) and away from the track.

Cross this and follow the wall on your right; ignore the first stile on

Windgather Rocks: a prominent sight from miles around

the left, but continue to the next stile. Cross it and turn immediately left, now keeping the wall/fence on your left.

On this section, the view ahead takes in Charles Head and the white buildings on Sponds Hill, above Lyme Park, while to the right you should see Jenkin Chapel, the Tors Ridge and Windgather Rocks, further left.

Cross another stile and continue downhill until almost at the bottom, where you swing right before a swampy and reedy area with a stream (Moss Brook) on your left. Cross the stream just before the point at which it meets the wall (4) in the bottom right-hand corner of the field, then cross a stile with a waymark. Cross a smaller stream and continue, in roughly the same direction as before, with the wall on your left. Keep above the reedy area and join an old green track, soon coming to a very wet section. Squelch your way through a mini-bog to a choice of two stiles. Cross the left-hand one, squelch through more bog, and pass a crumbling wall and an overgrown hawthorne. Continue to dry land with a wall on your right-hand side. Cross a further stile and then head towards farm buildings. Be sure to follow the main track, passing through two gates and near to the farm buildings, to the road (5). (Do not be tempted by an almost parallel path that swings away to the right, and which will entail more road walking.)

Cross the busy road with care then cross, in quick succession, a stile, a

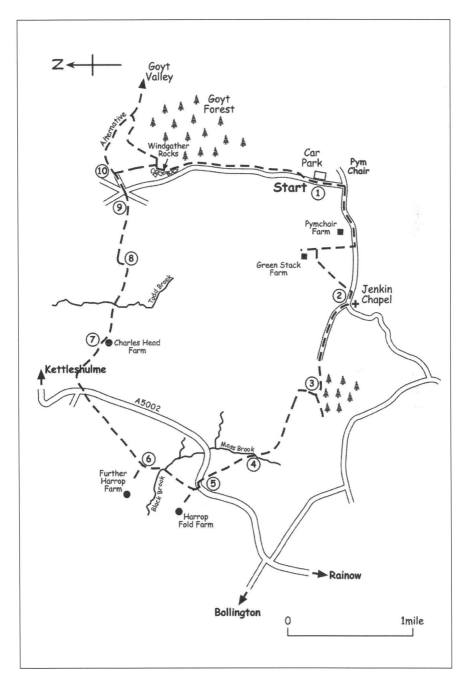

small field and another stile, after which you turn right and cross another stile just a few yards away, adjacent to a gate. Now, follow a wide grassy track downhill firstly with the wall on your right, down to the valley and across Black Brook. From here, continue up the track and, at the top of the uphill stretch, turn right (6), and follow a wall on your left for a short distance. After about 50m (ignore gate on right), fork right and follow a wide green track between trees; there are several such tracks around here and I've been told that they were part of a system of drove roads for cattle in past years. The track soon becomes boggy and narrower. You cross a stile, then a stream and continue ahead and upstream, being forced to walk to the left and above an overgrown sunken path.

Before a fence, plunge down to an improved track, cross a stile and walk up to the road (B5470). Cross the road and continue along the track, towards Charles Head Farm (7).

> The northerly views, to your left, are particularly impressive on this stretch of the walk. On a clear day, Whaley Moor, Chinley Churn and Kinder Scout can be seen.

Pass to the right of a modern house, then left of the renovated farm buildings, and follow a rough downhill track (and cobbles) to a stile. From here, head straight down the hill and left of a barn to a footbridge over Todd Brook. As you walk down this hill, Windgather Rocks are prominent on the skyline – and that's where you're heading!

Cross the bridge, turn left and head uphill, just to the right of a clump of trees. Then, aim just to the right of an old house which is straight ahead. Turn left, through a gateway, with the house on your left (8), and head for the next house. Go through a gateway and turn right along a track to the right of this house, and to the left of a barn.

Continue straight ahead (and mostly up!) towards the farm buildings to the left of Windgather.

> A few years ago, I met a man rebuilding part of a dry-stone wall here. After a health scare, he had retired from commerce and decided to pursue his loves of walking, climbing and wall building instead – quite a change in life-style, and one that he never regretted.

Cross a stile and turn left here to the appropriately-named Fivelane Ends (9). Cross the road junction, then fork right along a signposted track. You approach a restored farm on the left (10) – nowadays there are many of these, as small farms become uneconomic and redevelopment is a profitable option, fuelled by a boom in property prices. The shortest route from this point is to turn right almost opposite the house along a right of way that leads gently uphill and almost due south towards Windgather Rocks. But there is an alternative, slightly longer route which gives you an excellent view across the Goyt Valley. For this option, continue past the house, through a gate, alongside a wall on your left and straight ahead to a large tree by the wall corner. Here, cross a stile, turn right and continue – following the wall on your right – to the end of the field, then cross another stile. Your route would normally turn sharp right here, over a stile and into a conifer wood but, before doing so, if the weather is good, just keep going for a few more paces for the view over the top of the hill – quite a breathtaking prospect.

> This must have been a much-loved place as, on one visit here, there were some faded roses in a milk bottle with a card that read "Happy Birthday Dad – 15 July".

Having shared the enjoyment – photographs taken, or the view simply admired – return to your route and follow the path through the wood, keeping close to the wall on your right. When you meet the next wall, turn left and again keep this wall on your right, until – finally – you reach Windgather Rocks.

By whichever route you arrived here, perhaps having paused to admire the skills of rock climbers, follow the signed and stiled path in a southerly direction alongside the road, all the way back to your car.

Walks: KR5 & KR6

Lamaload, Forest Chapel, Shutlingsloe (optional), Cat and Fiddle and the Tors

Starting Point: Car park, east of Lamaload Reservoir, SJ976753

How to get there: see walk KR2

Map: OS Explorer OL 24 – The Peak District, White Peak Area

Length: 7 miles or 11 miles

Grade: Moderate

Duration: three hours or five hours

Walking in this area is enhanced by the many fine hills – a fact that would not have been appreciated quite as much by the men and horses taking salt across this rugged area from Northwich to Yorkshire. Saltersford, the name of a local hamlet, is derived from this trade; the men leading the horses were called 'salters' (funnily enough) or 'jaggers'. This term can still be found in Jagger's Clough, a few miles away; the name is derived from *jaeger*, the breed of horse preferred for this work.

The paths used on these walks are among the most frequented in the area. Certainly, they are popular, but with good reason – they comprise a classic pair of walks, each starting at Lamaload. Walk KR5 is the shorter one and is ideal for an afternoon stroll of three to four hours. Walk KR6 involves a little more hill climbing, but with fine views to reward you. The first part of each walk, as far as Forest Chapel, is the same, so you can always change your mind about the route to follow when you reach the chapel. To give you a third choice, you can also do just the second half of the walk, planning your own link between Forest Chapel and the Cat and Fiddle.

Remember – both walks start at the same place and cover the same ground as far as Forest Chapel, so the first part of the description is the same. *Also* – the final part of the route is the same; only the middle sections differ!

Walks KR5 and KR6 – first part of both walks

From the car park (1), go back to the road, turn right and walk along the road for about half a mile to a gate on the right with a notice telling you that this is a concessionary path, before the road starts to drop down. Go through the gate and follow the winding path to a track, where you turn right (2). Go along the track, until you arrive at a building on your right (remains of Lower Ballgreave Farm). Turn left off the track here and climb uphill to the remnants of a dry-stone wall. Turn left here, keeping the wall on your left, and head for the next ruined farm (Higher Ballgreave Farm). Keep to the right of the buildings, and then follow the lower (downhill) track.

At a stream (4), go through the gate and turn right. Go through two more gateways and, as you look ahead and slightly left, you will see a ruined building. Follow a path uphill to the ruin (5), which may soon become a heap of stones, and pause for a moment to look back to Lamaload and the distant moors to the north.

Now continue in the same direction to a gateway; go through this and head to the top-right-hand corner of the field, with Shutlingsloe ahead. Climb over the ladder stile, cross the main road, turn right and then immediately left along a short stretch of country lane. At the end, turn left along a road and continue until you reach a track (6) to Greenways Farm. Turn right here and, at the farm ahead, turn left behind the farmhouse. Cross the stile in the wall ahead of you. Go downhill (waymark) to a group of hawthorne bushes and cross the stile to the left of them, also crossing a small stream (7).

From here go uphill, and continue straight ahead, crossing a stile, and carrying on to a further clump of hawthorne. The path now continues straight ahead – soon with Shutlingsloe as a distant waymark – and eventually leads to a track near to Macclesfield Forest Chapel (8).

The tiny chapel dates back to 1673. Rush-bearing services take place here and at nearby Jenkin Chapel. In the case of Forest Chapel, the churchyard is left uncut until the rush-bearing event, which encourages a proliferation of wild flowers. According to a notice in the entrance, around 70 varieties of flowers are found in and around the churchyard – including mountain pansies, sweet cicely and poppies; I've spotted some, but not all!

From the chapel, there are two possible routes for you to choose; the short route is described first, the longer one second. *The final part of each route is the same and is at the end of this route description headed 'Main Route'.*

Macclesfield Forest Chapel in a patch of late afternoon sun

Short Route (KR5)

For the shorter route, where the path meets the track referred to above, turn left – i.e. away from the chapel and in a westerly direction. (If you have visited the chapel, turn left as you leave it.) Continue down the track, turn left at a T-junction with a lane, and, at the bottom of the hill (9), turn left again at a T-junction with the more major road in Wildboarclough. After about 100m, at 'Bottom-of-the-Oven', turn right along a tarmac track, and across a stream. Go through a farmyard, following the signs, and out through two gates to go uphill, with a wall on your left. The next stile is in the top-left corner of the field (10).

Cross a stile and bear left (45°) to a ladder stile. Cross this and turn right, to keep the wall on your right. Cross a stone step-stile, then go straight ahead, downhill, to a broad track between two offset walls. Turn left here (11) and follow the direction of the Public Footpath sign towards the buildings of Torgate Farm, keeping the wall on your left. A few hundred metres before the farm, cross a ladder stile.

From here, continue for 100m to a sign for a concessionary footpath (12). There is (or was) a map on the post, but this, briefly, is what you do: turn right and follow the waymarks downhill. The route soon peels away

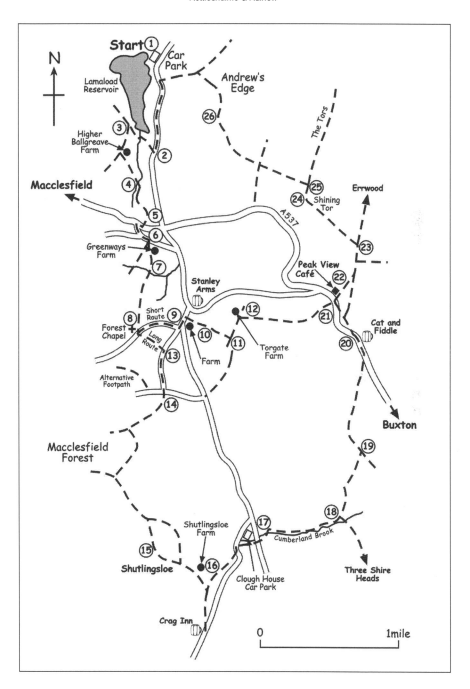

to the right and crosses the stream in a dip called Chest Hollow. Continue ahead to cross a stile by a gate and follow the broad green track uphill, with a stream on your right, all the way to the main (A537) road (21). The route is clearly waymarked.

Cross the main road, then walk leftwards along the access road that leads to the Peak View café and restaurant. Just before the café, turn right and follow the signed track that crosses a stile about 50m before Stake Farm (22). *Continue straight ahead, cross one more stile and you join the main route. To complete this shortened route, skip the next section and proceed to 'Main Route'.*

Longer Route – middle section (KR6)

For the longer route, turn right along the track and pass the chapel (8) on your right, then take the first left turn and proceed to the T-junction (13). Turn right here and walk up the steep road as far as a T-junction (14). Go straight ahead at the junction, along a concessionary bridleway that eventually leads into the forest and towards the ruins of 'Ferriser' – perhaps this was once connected with the blacksmith's trade, but not even Google can shed any light on the origin of the word.

About half a mile beyond the building, you reach a viewpoint with views through the forest towards Trentabank Reservoir and Tegg's Nose. After a further few hundred metres, towards the top of the hill, turn left up some steps to a stile. Beyond the stile, the footpath is signposted to 'Wildboarclough via Shutlingsloe Farm'. The track is very obvious, being surfaced with stone slabs to combat erosion. After a stretch of duckboarding, cross a stile and you have a choice: the path ahead leads you around Shutlingsloe and might be a good choice in bad weather; otherwise, turn right and follow the path to the top of Shutlingsloe (15).

I'm told that the farmer used to take pot shots at ramblers on 'his hill' long before the right of way was established! Nowadays, you can admire the view in peace – locating distant hills with the help of the handy toposcope.

The path goes straight over the top and heads downhill towards Shutlingsloe Farm. Keep to the right of the farm and go down a tarmac track as far as a cattle grid before a green metal sign, and turn sharp left along a track (16) past Bank Top and down to a road, which you cross to a bridge almost opposite. Cross this and follow the path which leads to the right of a farmhouse. Go through the farmyard, bear right and cross the road to a gateway (17), signposted 'Public Footpath to Cat and Fiddle

A fine day at The Cat and Fiddle – it's not always like this!

Inn'. Take this path, crossing Cumberland Brook by way of a narrow bridge and continue uphill until you reach a T-junction of paths (18). On your right is a waterfall (in damp weather), but you turn left along a slightly less-well-worn track. The path goes uphill, first to the right and then to the left of a stream. Continue uphill in the same direction, eventually bearing right to a T-junction of paths by a Peak District & Northern Footpath sign (19). Take a left turn here along an obvious path that takes you to the Cat and Fiddle, the second-highest pub in England. On a clear day, the views from this path are unbeatable; the beer's quite good too.

From the pub, head north (i.e. towards Macclesfield) along the main road. Just after a bend to the left, you fork right (20) along a well-used track which used to be the main road – spot the milestone with distances to both Macclesfield and London!

The track leads towards the Peak View café (21) but, unless you want to visit the café, bear right at a fork in the track, and continue along this very popular route, with Stake Farm (22) on your left. You join the main route beyond a stile.

Main Route

This is where the long and short routes join – i.e. on the track with Stake Farm and the Peak View café behind and to the south-west. The path lies straight ahead, with a wall on your left, which is the boundary between Cheshire and Derbyshire. Continue to a kissing gate with a signpost to Shining Tor. Fine views will reward you on a good day: when the thermals are rising, you should see a fair number of hang-gliders on the western slopes of the Tors and, at one particular point, you'll glimpse Errwood Reservoir to the east (your right).

At the top of Shining Tor (24), the trig point on your left denotes the highest point in Cheshire. Access is concessionary. Having admired it, continue for 150m to a stile on your left (25), signposted to Lamaload Reservoir. Go in this direction, crossing one stile *en route* and always keeping the wall on your left.

> Trig points are no longer needed by surveyors, but they are greatly appreciated as landmarks. So why not give this one a hug to show that we still love him (or her)?

The path continues across the moorland initially almost due east, veers northwards and gives excellent views of Cats Tor on your right (the name is said to come from the packs of wild cats that inhabited the moors – you may find a better derivation).

Continue along the path until you reach the top of the hill (26), from where you'll have a fine view of Lamaload on your left and Windgather Rocks away towards the right. The path then goes downhill, crossing a stile. Continue down the hill, passing the sparse ruins of Eaves Farm on your right. Follow the path further downhill, with a small stream and fence on your left, until you meet the road. Turn right here and walk back to the car park at Lamaload Reservoir.

Walk: KR7

Todd Brook Circular: Pym Chair, Dunge Valley Gardens, Saltersford

Starting Point: Pym Chair car park SJ995767

How to get there: Easiest to drive to Kettleshulme on the B5470 and look for the sign near the school, pointing to Goyt Valley and Dunge Valley Gardens

Map: OS Explorer OL 24 – The Peak District, White Peak Area

Length: 7 miles

Grade: Easy/Moderate (except for the walk back to the car park!)

Duration: Three hours

The area between Rainow and Kettleshulme represents the best of East Cheshire hill country: lonely, sometimes bleak, but with its own rugged beauty and occasional surprises.

Walk out of the car park, turn left and then right at the T-junction. Head downhill and westwards until the road levels out just after Pymchair Farm, then turn right at a footpath sign (1) over two stiles towards the renovated Green Stack Farm. Keep to the right of the buildings (2) then follow the footpath straight ahead, keeping to the left of the wall. The path crosses a stile to a substantial stone barn. Bear slightly right with a house in the distance and a road a little to the right. Go through an area that's often squelchy and towards a group of trees. Cross a stile to the left of mixed woodland and then head downhill for a short distance to a second stile (3) towards Dunge Valley Gardens, based on what was Dunge Farm.

> From spring to autumn, the gardens here are a fine sight. For a modest admission charge you can visit the main gardens which stretch to the rear of the house. Currently (2010) opening hours are restricted to 10.30am to 5pm Thursday, Friday, Saturday, Sunday and Bank Holiday Mondays.from March to June For further information, check the website – www.dungevalley.co.uk.

Cross a stream and continue on the right of way, keeping the lawn of the house on your right. Follow the track and climb uphill to a cattle grid

A glimpse of Dunge Valley Gardens

with a footpath sign, where you turn left (4), passing a house (Tunstead Knoll Farm) and stables on your right. Pass through a gate, then turn left and head downhill to a disused building (5). Cross a stile here then pass a further stile, nearby on your left, leading you across a field and across a stream – it's easiest over a well-used route with shallow water and improvised stepping stones. The stream is a tributary of Todd Brook, and we cross the brook much later in the walk.

After this, go uphill, turn right and find the stile by the gate. Turn left here and go straight ahead for 20m or so then follow a row of trees running parallel to a wall away to your left. Go through a gate and along a grassy track. As this bends to the left, just before a hawthorne bush atop a grassy mound, fork right and cross Todd Brook by a bridge. Head towards the house (Summer Close), and pass just below it to join the farm track. Turn left and then almost immediately right to slant uphill along a clear – initially sunken – track that lies a little to the right.

Some way before the top of the hill, another path veers left, but just keep the wall on your left and continue to the top. Pause to admire, on your extreme left, Windgather Rocks, which run south to Cats Tor and Shining Tor – the highest point in Cheshire. Having arrived at the top,

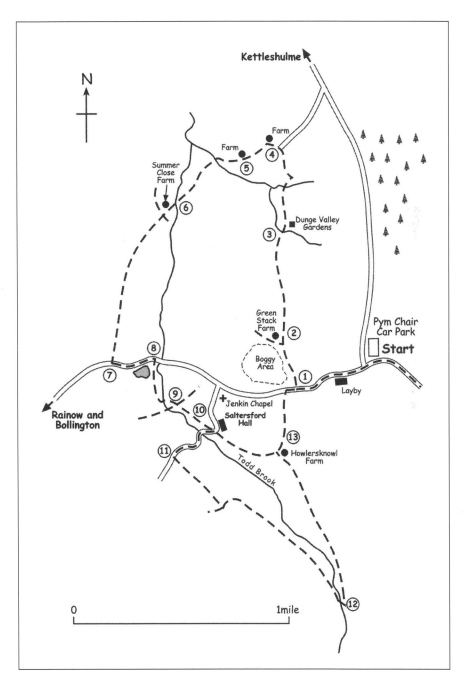

Kettleshulme

N

Farm

Farm

4

5

Summer
Close
Farm

6

Dunge Valley
Gardens

3

Green
Stack
Farm

2

Pym Chair
Car Park

Start

8

Boggy
Area

1

Layby

7

Rainow and
Bollington

9

Jenkin Chapel

10

Saltersford
Hall

13

11

Howlersknowl
Farm

Todd Brook

0   1mile

12

continue across the plateau and through three stiles to an eroded track, where you turn left (7) down 'The Corkscrew'.

Continue downhill, the track widening somewhat and eventually becoming a narrow cobbled lane. At the bottom of the hill, go past the pool belonging to the house on your right, then turn immediately right through a gate (8). This permissive path makes for a pleasanter route than the right of way through the property. Having gone through the gate, go straight ahead and find a stile a little to the right and then head towards a stone barn. Cross a stile, then a footbridge (9), keeping Todd Brook on your right until you reach the road (10).

From here, you have a choice – stay with me for the complete walk and enjoy a meander towards the headwaters of Todd Brook, or go past Saltersford Hall Farm straight to Howlersknowl Farm (13), from where you would turn left and head north to rejoin my recommended path. This might be handy if – heaven forbid – the weather turns foul.

For those accompanying me, turn right on the road and head uphill. As the road levels out, turn left (11) along a farm track. Immediately before the farm, go through a gateway and turn left, keeping the wall on your left. Cross two stiles and head for the far right corner of the field. Cross a stile here and go straight ahead, following the contour of the hill.

Where the path meets the junction of three old walls, begin to head downhill – the seemingly unpromising route develops into a more obvious path as it eventually descends gently to cross a stile just above a stream. Continue in the same direction, keeping well to the right of the more prominent stream – Todd Brook again! Very eventually, the path crosses a stile in a wall and leads to a track crossing Todd Brook (12). (For purists: the right of way is actually a few metres further on.)

Follow the path for a few metres past the scant remains of a ruined building: turn left and follow the obvious track northwards. This continues straight ahead, at first climbing gently with Todd Brook now on your left. Eventually, it runs alongside (either side) of a wall and then follows a clear track downhill towards Howlersknowl Farm (13); *this is where the short-cut from Saltersford Hall Farm joins the main route.* From here, skirt around the right-hand edge of the buildings, through two stiles and a gate, after which you turn right and head north again along the driveway. At the road, turn right and return – up a hill that seems steeper than when you came down it just 3 hours ago – to your car.

PRESTBURY

Prestbury has two faces. To some, it is the quaint main street with up-market shops and an inevitable upper-crust image. But it is also an historic village of great charm, lying in some of the most beautiful Cheshire countryside. This is the perfect combination for walking: some hills to make the walk worthwhile, but a lush greenness so often lacking in the wilder areas further east.

About the Village

The village takes its name from the Saxon 'Preost burgh', or Priest's Town. The first settlement was made around AD670 by missionary priests. In fact, one of our walks begins in Priest Lane, just to emphasise the monastic influence. St Peter's Church is the most notable building in the village, with a Norman chapel nearby, on the south-east side. A further priestly connection is the 15th-century Priest's House, a black-and-white building in the village centre, now the National Westminster Bank. The vicar is said to have addressed his parishioners from the balcony on this building on one occasion during the Commonwealth, when the church was closed to him by the Puritans.

The main street in Prestbury, with the ancient 'Priest's House'

St Peter's, Prestbury

Like many villages in Cheshire, Prestbury became associated with weaving. In Prestbury's case, it was silk, as it was on a much larger scale in nearby Macclesfield. The silk merchants used to drive their wagons across the Bollin, which flows through Prestbury, by way of a ford. This is still remembered today in the name of Ford House which is near to the bridge built from the profits of the silk trade. But for a local benefactor, it is claimed that Ford House might have become a casino!

That is as much as we can say about the village itself in this short space. The parish of Prestbury is, surprisingly, one of the largest in England. Next time you are driving around this area, just see how far the Prestbury boundary signs extend. Even Tytherington, which most people think of as being in Macclesfield, is part of the parish of Prestbury.

Surprisingly, I can't find a comprehensive website for Prestbury from where you might get further information – just the rather good one for the local church (www.stpetersprestbury.org.uk), an interesting transcript of a local history lecture (www.prestburycheshire.com/cartmell.htm) and a couple for the local restaurants.

The Walks

The footpath routes around Prestbury are such that it is difficult to work out more than three or four decent circular walks which begin in Prestbury village. Some paths also end on busy main roads, necessitating occasional lengthy road walking. The walks to be described are, however, a good selection for this highly attractive area.

Walk: P1

Mottram Cross to Adder's Moss

Starting Point: Priest Lane, SJ876785

How to get there: Priest Lane is almost opposite Mottram Cross, on the Mottram to Prestbury road; it runs alongside the Italian restaurant (was the Bull's Head) towards Mottram St Andrew primary school. Park near the warning sign for the school; the road is wider here and is the safest place to park.

Map: OS Explorer 268 – Wilmslow, Macclesfield & Congleton

Length: 3 miles

Grade: Easy

Duration: One and a half hours

Although this short walk begins in Mottram St Andrew, it qualifies for this section as it's nearer to Prestbury than any other major centre. The countryside here is just hilly enough to be interesting without being exhausting – almost as though the fields have been tipped up for you to admire. It's an ideal walk before (or after!) a Sunday lunch.

From the recommended parking place, walk back to the footpath sign opposite to Priest Cottage and cross the stile (1). Go along a track and turn right at the end of it, heading uphill. Continue straight ahead to the road, climbing one stile *en route*. The stile to the road is in the far corner of the field, beside a house (2). Turn left at the road, and walk

Mottram Cross, almost opposite the Italian restaurant

past Goose Green Farm on your right. After about a quarter of a mile, turn right into a field (3) through a kissing gate opposite to the first farm on your left.

The path crosses the field, heading slightly right and then downhill to a stile that is not visible from the road. Cross the next field at an angle of about 45°, heading to a point mid-way between two woods. The larger wood (on the left) is Alder Wood, and you should not be tempted to head for the stile that is at the far left of this wood. The path that you need is less obvious: it goes towards the *right* of Alder Wood (4), then dips down and through a gate into the wood itself. Walk along this National Trust permissive path through the wood, ignoring the bridge over the stream (except perhaps to explore the delights of this attractive woodland) and emerge through a stile at the other end. Turn left from here along a well-worn field track and continue parallel to Daniel Hill Wood, about 100m to your right. The track eventually passes through Mount Farm to the road.

Turn right at the road then right again (5) along the access lane for the properties ahead. Bear right at the gate to Adder's Moss Farm, and continue along the track, which eventually leads past Hill Top Farm on your far right. Much further to your right, you can glimpse the hills above Rainow and Kettleshulme – fine walking country for another day.

Where the farm drive turns right, continue ahead to cross a stile into a field. In a hundred metres or so, there is a stile (6) on your left; you can climb over this for a small diversion to Waterfall Wood – follow the sound of running water and you'll see how the wood got its name. After the diversion, or if you're just carrying on, continue walking along the edge of the field for another 100m to a pond by a large tree. Turn right here and pass a much larger pond on your left, then keep walking to the top of the hill and cross a stile.

Turn left, then almost immediately turn right to head steeply downhill (7) through a wood. The route soon levels out and you keep straight ahead, over the stiles, with the hedge on your left. Soon, in the extreme left corner of a field, cross a footbridge over a stream then continue past a pond and cross another footbridge. From here, still with the hedge on your left, keep going until you reach the road (8), where you turn right. At the first road junction, turn right again to walk along Priest Lane and head back to where you started.

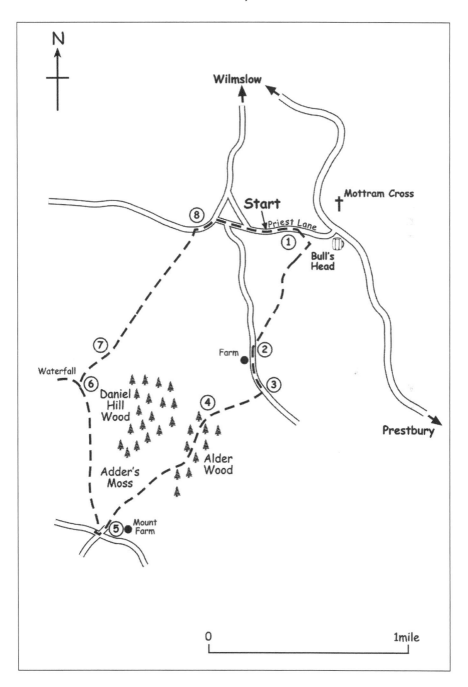

Walk: P2
Prestbury to Mottram

Starting Point: Springfields car park in Prestbury (behind the Admiral Rodney) SJ902773.

How to get there: at the north end of the village, past the restaurants and on the opposite side of the road from the church.

Map: OS Explorer 268 – Wilmslow, Macclesfield & Congleton

Length: 6 miles

Grade: Easy/Moderate

Duration: Two and a half hours

This walk never strays far away from the River Bollin, and follows part of the Bollin Valley Way. The only problem, wherever the Bollin is concerned, is that the soft river banks are being constantly eroded. Since the 2007 version of this book, this walk has been badly affected by erosion in two places which I will deal with as we reach them!

From the starting point, walk north through the car park, past the bungalows. Turn left along Scott Road, then right into Bollin Grove. Continue past the football pitch to the end of the tarmac, after which a track continues to the River Bollin. Walk alongside the Bollin, following the signpost pointing to Wilmslow. Do not cross the bridge, just go straight ahead – also passing the sewage works, so keep moving!

Problem #1: in May 2010, this path was closed for at least six months; there may be a temporary diversion by the time you read this.

After the very end of the sewage complex, the waymarked path continues through the fields and stays near to the Bollin, with some spectacularly eroded banks. On reaching a bridge (1), do not cross it but head for the top-right-hand corner of the field. Climb the stile, and follow the waymark towards the middle of the farm (Top o' th' Hill) facing you (2). Pass between the farm buildings and almost immediately turn left over a stile, and walk parallel to the road on your right. The path eventually switches to the right of the hedge-line. Keep close to the hedge, continue across a footbridge and stiles, across a final stile, then turn right to join a drive that continues to the main road (3).

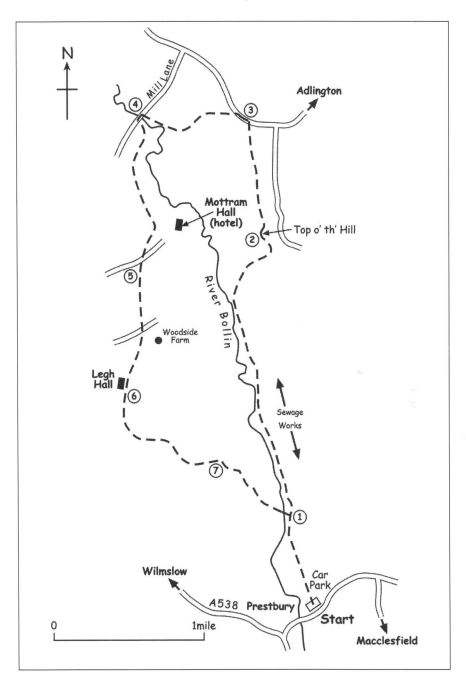

The view across the golf course to Mottram Hall Hotel and club house

Turn left at the road, then go over the stile (signposted 'Mill Lane') to the right of a drive. The path heads slightly to the right, then through a gate and a series of stiles (be sure to cross each one, as one of them switches you to the other side of the hedge). The path is clearly waymarked, with a final swing to the right at a footpath sign that leads to Mottram Bridge, the road bridge (4) that is clearly visible a little to the right. Cross the stile onto Mill Lane, and turn left across Mottram Bridge.

Problem #2: My route used to turn immediately left again here, upstream, but the path has collapsed into the river and the landowner appears to be unlikely to agree to a re-routing of the right of way. What to do, other than get your feet wet?

Temporary solution: the owners of Mottram Hall Hotel have proposed a temporary concessionary route on their own land linking to where a new bridge is planned to be built across the Bollin further upstream. Until the bridge has been built, this is the temporary route:

Having joined Mill Lane and turned left across Mottram Bridge, continue for about 200m to a wide gateway on the left-hand side. Cross the fence adjacent to the gate and walk across the field, keeping a line of mature trees on your right. Walk under cables to a wide gateway at the far corner. Turn right through a kissing gate then along a well-waymarked route towards Mottram Hall Hotel. Pass a football pitch on the left and head to the left of the clubhouse; circle around the building to a signpost, then follow waymarks to the corner of the golf course and across the hotel drive to the next signpost, crossing iron railings via a stile (5).

If this concessionary route is impassable for any reason , walk along Mill Lane for a further 300m or so to a ladder stile with a Bollin Valley Way sign. Cross the stile, ignore the waymark arrow and, instead, go through the gate on your left and turn right to follow the service road to the hotel drive which you walk down to the stile on the right across the iron railings.

From here, continue ahead and over a small rise towards Woodside Farm. At the driveway to the nearby cottage, which is on the left, turn right and walk to the gateway (a small diversion from the right of way, suggested by the landowner to avoid the farmyard). Go straight ahead from the gateway, with the farm wall on your left.

From here, head up through the fields towards Legh Hall; the path starts on the right of the hedge but, after 100m, crosses over to the left at a stile. Continue to a kissing gate to Legh House, then walk along the walled drive to Legh Hall (6), then turn left along a track.

Enter the circular tarmac area belonging to the large converted coach house and go through the kissing gate into a field. Follow the waymarked route downhill and continue downhill to a stile. Follow the edge of the next field, over another stile and carry on towards the right of the farm facing you. Turn left at the farm drive and then continue down the track to the Little Gadhole group of buildings.

Follow the waymarks, pass a pool on your left, then turn right at a waymark. From here, the rest of the route is obvious. It drops down, through a stile, to a footbridge (7), then round to the right and over another stile. Turn left and follow the hedge, with Spittle House on your left.

The original 14th/15th-century building is believed to have been a primitive hospital run by the church, possibly for the benefit of lepers and others deemed to be kept away from the rest of society.

Bear left to a stile that leads to the drive to the house, and then turn right along the drive. Continue down to cross the bridge over the River Bollin, then turn right and head for home.

Walk: P3

Prestbury to Whiteley Green

Starting Point: Springfields car park in Prestbury (behind the Admiral Rodney) SJ902773

How to get there: at the north end of the village, past the restaurants and on the opposite side of the road from the church.

Map: OS Explorer 268 – Wilmslow, Macclesfield & Congleton

Length: 4½ miles

Grade: Easy/Moderate

Duration: Two hours

This is a varied walk, including some gentle hills which give good views of 'real' hills just a few miles away. Unfortunately, there are a few roads to cross because a few years ago, the A523 was re-routed as part of a major road project and has sliced through several footpaths in the area. Do not rely on an OS map unless it shows the new road network. On the other hand, you'll also walk along part of the old road from Butley Town towards Bollington – now, scarcely a cart track.

Walk towards the centre of Prestbury (i.e. the reverse of the way you drove into the car park) and turn right along the main road, passing the Admiral Rodney. Turn left into Bridge Green and after about 100m, turn right (1) along a grassy track signposted 'Bollin Valley Way'. Walk between the River Bollin and the back gardens of the houses, then keep to the path by the garden fences (i.e. ignore the tempting little footbridge) and rejoin the road at a turning circle.

Keep straight on (ignore the turn to the right) and go through the tunnel under the railway. Bear slightly right to follow the direction of the next footpath sign across a field and, soon after crossing a plank bridge in the middle of the field, cross a stream. Follow a path with the stream on your left until you come to a stile. Cross this, turn right and, soon afterwards, go left over the next stile.

You are now on Tytherington golf course (2). From here, the scenery begins to unfold, with Prestbury behind you, and the hills beyond Bollington ahead. As you walk along this path, Kerridge Hill is slightly to your left, with White Nancy sitting on Kerridge's left-most 'knee'.

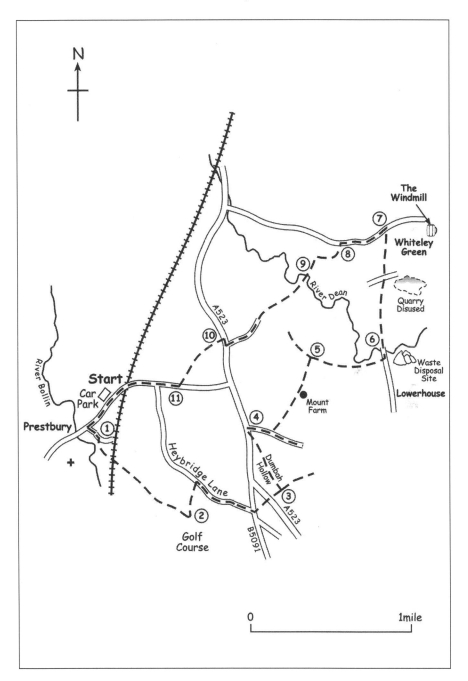

New Road, Prestbury – paradise for gastronomes

Keep the perimeter fence on your left, and eventually you pass a signpost, pointing right to Macclesfield. Continue ahead until the right of way goes to the left, between the perimeter fence and a flimsier affair. Walk between these two fences, then turn left on a tarmac track and continue to Heybridge Lane.

> The word 'Heybridge' is said to be a corruption of the old English for 'High Birches'.

Turn right and walk up the lane to what was the A523 but is now the B5091 (London Road); there's also the new A523 (the Silk Road), which means that we now have not one, but two major roads slicing through the footpaths around here. Cross London Road, turn right, then first left at the footpath sign, up the drive to 'Dumbah'. After passing the large house on your right, the tarmac drive heads downhill towards 'Old Dumbah'. Just before this house, cross a stile on your left and turn right towards a footpath sign. Cross a stile and go down a flight of steps to the A523 – a very busy main road. Cross with great care, go up a flight of steps and turn left (3) along a right of way running parallel to the road. Continue in a straight line above Dumbah Hollow – an attractive and popular little walking area blighted by the noise of nearby traffic. Leave the path by two flights of steps and turn right (4) along the road to Bollington.

After 100m, turn left and walk along the drive to Mount Farm – leaving the traffic behind. Walk past the farm buildings, keeping them on your right. About 150m after the farmhouse, turn right (5). (The stile to the left leads to a section of what was the old road from Butley Town to Bollington – long before Prestbury assumed its present importance.)

Having turned right, keep the fence on your right and carry on along the 'old road' towards Bollington – you'll see White Nancy straight ahead. About half way along this track, turn left over a stile and head towards a wooded area. Go through this to the bank of the River Dean, turn right and follow the river upstream. After crossing a jumble of stiles, footbridge and steps, the path bears right across a field and heads towards a further stile, opposite to a large factory building (6). Turn left here and follow the road in the direction of the household waste site, crossing the Dean along the way.

Just left of the entrance gates to the household waste site, pass through a gate with a footpath sign. Carry on in a straight line for two-thirds of a mile, until you reach the road at Whiteley Green (7). Along the way, cross a track serving the disused Whiteley Green Quarry and on the final stretch, with a large farm complex to your right, bear right; the stile onto the road is just to the left of the farm.

Turn left at the stile, and walk down the road for a quarter of a mile. Just after the road bends to the right, (about 30m after the quarry entrance) cross a stile by the second gate (8) on your left.

Follow the hedge, passing under the electricity cables, then go sharply left (still by the hedge) and cross a metal footbridge over the River Dean (9). From here, the path bears right to a stile in the top-right-hand corner of the field, to the right of a gate. A minor path diversion has taken place here: having crossed the stile, you now have to turn left and then right after a short distance, over another stile. Follow the wire fence (on your right) uphill to join the 'old' route which has been re-routed for no obvious reason. Pass through two large gates (a stile would be nice here), through the farmyard and left at a minor road. This leads through the hamlet of Butley Town to the main (A523) road.

Turn right and, after 50m or so, cross the road. Cross a stile to the right of a house (10) – though you may think about a diversion to the Butley Ash, just a few paces away. Our route, minus pub, is waymarked by the Bollin Valley Project. Start by keeping to the hedge on your left and, after the footbridge, turn slightly left and head for a white bungalow (11) peeping through the trees – the stile is nearly opposite it. Finally, turn right and head back to Prestbury.

Walk: P4

Prestbury, the Golf Course, Big Wood and Withinlee Road

Starting Point: car park near village hall, off Shirley's Drive SJ901768;

How to get there: starting from the mini-roundabout in the village, follow the Macclesfield road (B5087) and turn left at the 'P' sign.

Map: OS Explorer 268 – Wilmslow, Macclesfield & Congleton

Length: 4½ miles

Grade: Easy/Moderate

Duration: Two hours

Special note: of the 4½ miles, about one mile is on road. That's not a great problem, but there is a short and unavoidable quarter-mile along the busy A538 Prestbury/Wilmslow road *and I do not recommend this for a family group – especially with young children: you have been warned!* On the plus side, there are two lovely woods and many open views to enjoy for most of the walk.

Follow the 'pedestrians' signs from the car park into the village (1). Go to the mini-roundabout and pass Bridgfords (left) and Royles car dealers (right). After about 100m, turn left into Chelford Road and go uphill for about a quarter of a mile. Pass Collar House Drive (on the right) and just 50 paces later, go left through a kissing gate into the golf course (2).

This waymarked path begins by running alongside the right-hand edge of the course, and then down to Spencer Brook. From the brook, the path lies straight ahead. Continue to follow the marker posts – but where you enter a broad, open area of the course with a warning about golfers coming from the right, you need to check the onward route. Ahead and to the right you should be able to see where the next marker is, on the edge of a wood, and this is where you should head for. Soon after entering the wood, pass between a fence and trees.

At the tarmac drive (3) leading to the golf club, turn right, then left at a small flight of stone steps. This leads to a clearly defined and waymarked path, emerging at a minor road (4). Cross the road to a stile to the next public footpath. The path follows the right-hand edge of the playing field until it reaches a stile with three stone steps on your right. Cross this and

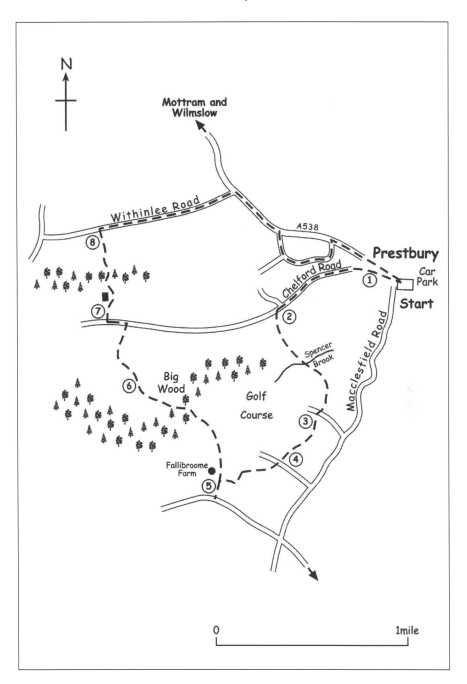

turn left. Follow the edge of the field and head towards Fallibroome Farm (5), crossing a further stile.

Follow a direction arrow and bear right (away from the farm) towards a stile near the corner of an adjacent field, and near a large tree. Do *not* cross the stile, but continue in the same general direction as you were walking (almost due north), as indicated by a further waymarker arrow. Head to a stile a few metres to the right of a gateway with stone gateposts. Cross the stile and continue, with a fence on your left.

Cross the next stile, re-entering the golf course for a short distance. Keep left along the edge of the course and cross a further stile. Bear slightly right towards Big Wood and cross the stile into the wood. A footbridge crosses the stream, taking you to a path that leads uphill and out of the wood, over a stile.

Go straight ahead, with the hedge on your right. In the top-right corner of the field (6), cross a stile, then almost immediately turn left over another, and walk to the right of the ancient hedge – now a line of near-mature trees – that is facing you. Your next stile is almost straight ahead, in a dip about 50m to the right of a gateway.

Cross the stile (and stream) and walk uphill with the hedge on your left. Be sure to look over your shoulder from the top of the hill – there is a splendid view, right over to the Peak District hills.

Turn left at the road (Chelford Road), then right after about 80m (7) along the drive to Crabtree Cottage. Just before the gate to the house itself, turn right through a wooden gate then left along a wide track for 50m or so, and left again at a wide gateway. Follow the waymarked path through a delightful area of mixed woodland, which includes numerous Scots Pine: my favourite tree.

Emerge onto Withinlee Road and turn right (8). Follow this relatively quiet road for about half a mile until you reach the Prestbury/Macclesfield road. Turn right here, **but be very careful indeed: *this is a very dangerous road. Car drivers along here seem oblivious to pedestrians and there are hardly any stretches of verge – make good use of the few bits you can find.*** After about a quarter of a mile, you reach Castle Gate (8) and from here you have a choice: either continue and use the pavement that begins in a few metres or escape from the traffic and follow Castle Gate in a loop that eventually leads you closer to Prestbury and its many eateries. Calm your shattered nerves with a visit to The Legh Arms or, further through the village, the Admiral Rodney.

SIDDINGTON & THE PEOVERS

Like many of the western areas covered in this book, Siddington and the various Peovers lie in rich dairy-farming and arable country.

Siddington is a sprawling parish with no real village centre. Its name derives from that of the de Sydington family who settled here in the time

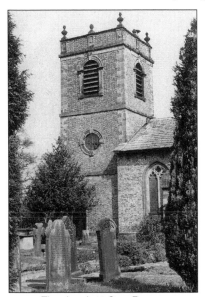

The church at Over Peover

of Henry III. The most notable place to visit in the area is Capesthorne Hall, home of the Bromley-Davenport family. Apart from the usual attractions of a stately home, there is a nature trail through the park, which will keep the children busy.

The Peovers comprise Higher Peover, Lower Peover and Peover Heath. You'll scarcely know where one ends and the next begins, and you may also be puzzled by the alternative names of Peover Superior, Peover Inferior and Nether Peover. But, it is well worth persevering. Peover Hall, in Higher Peover, was due for demolition, but it has been restored and is open to the public occasionally. It is accessed along a private drive leading from Grotto Lane which also leads to St Lawrence's, often referred to as Cheshire's Hidden Church. Further details are in Walk SP2.

Lower Peover's greatest claims to fame are the Bells of Peover Inn, and the almost adjacent St Oswald's Church. This contains a chest said to be carved from a single piece of oak. The lid is so heavy that it was used to assess the strength of any girl intending to wed a local farmer – obviously you needed a strong arm as well as a pretty face in those days.

The Walks

The walking around here is all of an easy nature. Not surprisingly, many of the footpaths are also farm drives so you'll see more than the usual amount of agriculture in this section of the book.

Walk: SP1

Redesmere, Siddington and Capesthorne

Starting Point: Car park adjacent to Redesmere, Fanshawe Lane, off the A34. SJ849713.

How to get there: Fanshawe Lane is off the A34, about 5 miles south of Alderley Edge and about 300m north of the crossroads with the B5392.

Map: OS Explorer 268 – Wilmslow, Macclesfield & Congleton

Length: 7 miles

Grade: Easy

Duration: Two and a half hours

Greedy ducks and noisy geese pose unusual hazards at the start, for both motorists and pedestrians. Apart from that, it's an easy walk through some of the fine farmland and farms of Cheshire. I've planned a clockwise route so that you can stop towards the end of the walk with a fabulous view of Capesthorne Hall – with the ducks sufficiently far away so as not to steal your picnic. Still with food in mind, there's often an ice-cream van at the car park and, even better, the excellent 'Coffee House and Brasserie' at Marton – check it's open by phoning 01260 224785. But first, the walk.

Leave your car at the parking area alongside Redesmere. Continue to walk along Fanshawe Lane, with the mere on your left. Pass Redesmere Cottage on the left, Hills Green Farm on your right, then turn right at the stile across the clear waters of Fanshawe Brook (1).

Climb the small incline and head through a waymarked line of stiles across the fields towards Hazelwall Farm (2). Cross the final fence before the property by way of

Out for a stroll: locals at Redesmere

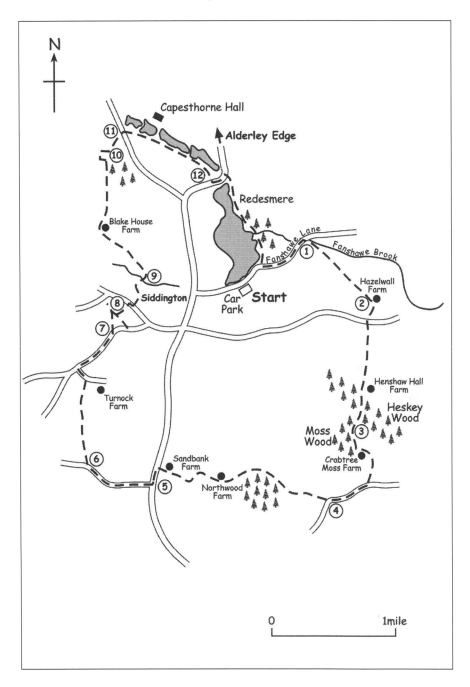

N

Capesthorne Hall

Alderley Edge

⑪

⑩

⑫

Redesmere

Blake House
Farm

Fanshawe Lane

Fanshawe Brook

①

Hazelwall
Farm

②

⑨

Siddington

⑧

Car
Park

Start

⑦

Turnock
Farm

Henshaw Hall
Farm

**Heskey
Wood**

**Moss
Wood**

③

⑥

Sandbank
Farm

Crabtree
Moss Farm

⑤

Northwood
Farm

④

0   1mile

a kissing gate and turn right on a diversion around the perimeter fence and then right at the drive.

Cross the B5392 road and walk along Henshaw Lane until you reach a fork. Follow the right fork to Henshaw Hall Farm and reach a huge barn conversion. The right of way was straight ahead but is now likely to be diverted around the property. Having done that, follow the track which soon leads down to Heskey Wood, then bears left (3) past Moss Wood.

The path now heads across a field towards Crabtree Moss Farm. As your route passes the end of a wood (Moss Wood), turn left and follow a path, with a hedge on your right, to the property. There have been major changes here, but all for the better – just follow the clear signs along a tarmac drive, now a bridleway. Turn right at the road, continue for about a quarter of a mile, then right again at a Public Footpath sign (4) onto a track which runs along the right-hand edge of a field. Pass two redundant stiles, continue on a track to the right of a wood, then pass through Northwood Farm (from which a path heads due north and saves about 3 miles) and then past Sandbank Farm (both working farms – quite unusual around here!) and back to the A34.

Turn left, walk along the verge of this busy road and turn right into Blackden Lane (5) as far as the first farm track on your right (6), signposted to Siddington. Join the track and continue straight ahead across a series of stiles until you arrive at the drive to Turnock Farm (the path joins the drive midway between Turnock Farm on your right and the house on your left). Turn left here and continue to the B5392 road, where you turn right and continue until Holly Cottage (7), which is on your left.

Fork left just after the cottage along a grassy track. Before you reach the next road (if you have done, turn back!), take a hairpin turn to the right (8) in front of two gateways. Follow this path for a short distance, then after 70m or so turn left – leading between tennis courts and a wood on your right.

Cross the road, turn right then left into Woodside (footpath sign). Note that the current OS maps incorrectly show the right of way *behind* the houses. Instead, proceed along Woodside (in front of the houses) and keep to the left, and pass in front of a group of bungalows, said to have been built by the Council across the original right of way – hence the OS confusion! After the bungalows, bear left onto a path into a wood. About 50m after crossing a stream, turn left at a footpath sign (9) along a delightful woodland path bounded by two hedges, eventually passing a thatched cottage and heading for Blake House Farm.

Capesthorne Hall, across the lake

To follow the right of way, turn right at the farm drive and follow it through the farmyard; alternatively, turn sharp right before the farmyard as suggested by a notice posted by the farmer. Both routes converge and you continue in the same direction, following a track which leads into a field with a fence on your right and a wood straight ahead.

Bear left across this field, towards its top-left-hand corner. Join a wide earthen track and, after a few metres, bear right off the track and cross fields by way of three stiles. Continue to a fourth stile, but do not cross this. Instead, turn left (currently, no waymark) and keep the hedge on your right. In just over 50m, turn right at a hedge corner and find the next stile tucked away in the hedge just before the next corner (10). Cross the next, immediately opposite, stile then go over a track and the stile facing you.

Traverse two fields, aiming for a small bungalow. Cross a minor road (11) and enter a field by way of the gate to the right of the bungalow. Keep to the left and continue past the lakes of Capesthorne Hall, soon with a classic view of the hall. Pass each lake then a wood on your left before you arrive at the A34. Cross this with care, turn left (12) and walk along the pavement, then right at the bridleway leading towards Redesmere. Follow the path around the lake back to your car.

Walk: SP2
Over Peover and Lower Peover

Starting Point: Clay Lane, Over Peover. SJ784735; this is a few minutes' walk from the entrance to the hall. The verges are wider here than other nearby lanes and you will cause less obstruction.

How to get there: Over Peover – the 'o' is silent – is about 4 miles south-east of Knutsford and can be accessed either along Stocks Lane from the A50, near Radbroke Hall, or along Pepper Street, Chelford.

Map: OS Explorer 268 – Wilmslow, Macclesfield & Congleton

Length: 9 miles

Grade: Easy

Duration: Four hours

From Clay Lane, walk down the lane (west) go over Grotto Lane, continue for a short distance on Goostrey Lane and turn right along the drive (1) towards the hall. As you approach the various estate buildings, bear right at a footpath sign and follow the sign to the car park.

> Peover Hall is an Elizabethan house dating from 1585. The house and gardens are open Mondays (but not Bank Holidays) and Thursdays 2.00 to 5.00pm from beginning of April to end of October. For further information, go to **www.peaksandplains.co.uk/directory/peover-hall-and-gardens**

Pass between various buildings and follow the sign that directs you past a walled garden to the Church of St Lawrence (normally locked). Parts may date from the 14th century but later additions include the brick-built 1739 tower and the nave and chancel, rebuilt in brick in 1811.

> One of its claims to fame is that General 'blood and guts' Patton had his wartime HQ in nearby Peover Hall and worshipped regularly at the church.

Facing the entrance to the church, follow a path between two lines of well-manicured beech trees. Pass an entrance to the gardens on the right and continue through the rhododendrons and mature trees of the Peover Estate. Leave the grounds through a kissing gate, turn left, and then right at the next stile (2). Keep the fence on your right, cross first one stile then another almost at the end of the field. Cross this and continue in the same direction as before, joining a track leading between mature horse chestnut trees to Stocks Lane (and the nearby Whipping Stocks pub).

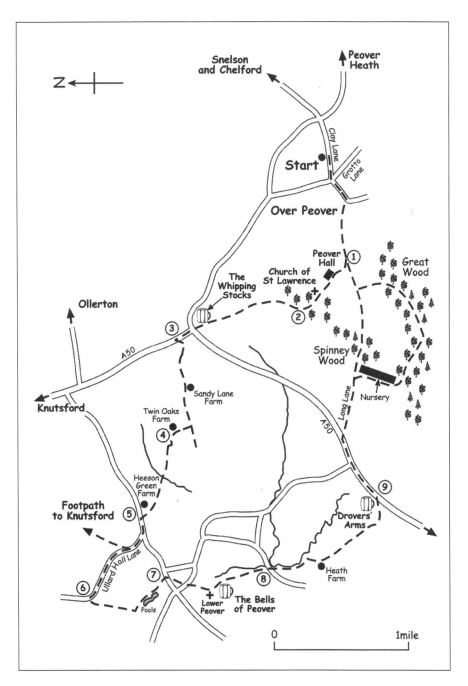

Cross the road and follow the A50 in the Knutsford direction, then take the first turn left (3) along a farm road with signs for a bridleway and a bed & breakfast. Keep left at a fork, go past Sandy Lane Farm on your left and take the next turn right to Twin Oaks Farm (4).

The route is well waymarked from here. As you approach a barn, turn left and follow the waymark to a stile. Cross this and keep to the right between Leylandii hedging. Continue, soon with a hawthorne hedge on your left, and cross the next stile. Walk across the field and go over a stile near the far-left corner. Cross the next field, go over a metal bridge over Red Brook and across a stile – then aim for the mid-point of the opposite hedge where a row of trees continues towards a farm. Climb over the stile at this point and follow the fence. The path passes an ornamental pond and goes through the farmyard, with noisy dogs, to the road (5).

Turn left here, then right along Ullard Hall Lane. Continue *past* Plumley Lane Farm (you can extend your walk by way of the footpath towards Knutsford which runs behind this farm). After a further quarter of a mile, turn left at a stile (6) as the road bears right.

Walk along the edge of the field until you reach a footpath sign, directing you across the 'prairie' created by merging several fields into one. After another 50m or so, bear slightly right towards a footpath sign. This is not exactly as shown by the OS, but much better than plodding around the edge of the field as was the case some years ago. Leave the prairie along a wide path between hedges. Cross a stile and walk along a well-maintained grassy area, past the house and onto the drive.

Just before the road (7) bear right past the display of garden furniture, cross the road and then the stile facing you. Follow the waymark, go over a stile then turn left after the next stile, then right, along a narrow lane (Barrows Brow) leading directly to St Oswald's church at Lower Peover.

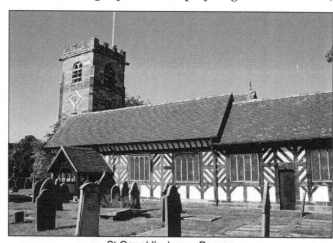

St Oswald's, Lower Peover

The earliest part of the church was built in 1269, making it the second-oldest timber-framed church in Europe – the oldest is at Marton. Many additions and changes were made over the centuries and a major restoration was completed in 1947. Well worth a visit – and the gravestones make interesting reading. The earliest one that I could spot was from the 17 century: "... departed this life April ye 14 1694".

From the churchyard gate by which you entered, follow the path to the left of the church. After leaving the churchyard, follow a path that bends to the right, heading for a wooded area and a river.

This is the oddly-named Peover Eye. I reckon the name is from Old English – 'peover' means 'bright' and 'ea' means 'river' so it simply means 'bright or shining river'.

Follow the river upstream until you meet the road (8) and cross the stile opposite. Follow the boundary fence by the river and continue across waymarked stiles. The well-walked path leads uphill, across yet more stiles and onwards until you reach the Drovers' Arms (9). Turn left and walk past the pub, along the A50 for half a mile until you reach Long Lane (watch for post-box) on your right.

After about 500m along Long Lane, immediately before a nursery with a vast number of greenhouses, it's decision time. **To chop almost a mile off the walk**, just carry on along the lane, but a more attractive route is as follows:

To complete the entire walk: turn right immediately before the nursery, walking along a track past greenhouses on your left. Pass a building and a further area of greenhouses and soon you see a footpath sign, seemingly leading directly into Spinney Wood. What this really means is that you turn left after the last greenhouse, then left again for about 50m to steps on the right that lead down to a footbridge into the wood. Follow the waymarks on an often mushy path with occasional boarding over some of the wettest bits. The path leads spasmodically alongside the Peover Eye and through Great Wood until you reach a bridge over the river. Do not cross this – instead, bear left uphill to a gate. Turn right, then left to rejoin Long Lane, where you turn right.

Carry on towards Peover Hall and either locate your car in the car park or retrace your steps to Clay Lane. If the latter, follow the bridleway sign at a junction and walk along the main drive – with yet more horse chestnut trees. They must be very fond of conkers around here!

WILDBOARCLOUGH

This is one of the most popular places to visit in east Cheshire. It gives easy access to a large area of surrounding hills and dales, though many visitors never stray far away from the Crag Inn, so it is rarely crowded. Currently, there is some debate as to whether this may change since there are suggestions from planners to build larger car parks and to 'develop' the area. I confess to having mixed feelings about this.

Historically, the name is derived from the supposedly last wild boar in England. Whether or not this is true, Wildboarclough was a surprisingly busy place when weaving was in its heyday. The old post office (with a claim to have been the largest sub post office in England) was part of Crag Mill, an 18th-century silk mill built in the grand Georgian style. There were several other busy mills, including nearby Gradbach Mill which manufactured flax and silk fabrics; nowadays, this mill has been lovingly restored as a youth hostel.

Another interesting area is the nearby Three Shire Heads (often called, incorrectly Three Shires Head – even on some OS maps) which is at the junction of Cheshire, Staffordshire and Derbyshire. Way back in the 14th century, Macclesfield Forest extended to here and local felons used to cross the border to make their getaway, after trapping animals in the forest. More recently, bare-knuckle boxing matches were held here illegally. As the Cheshire constabulary, for example, arrived, boxers and spectators would just step over the boundary into Derbyshire or Staffordshire.

The Walks

This is rugged walking country. You can easily leave the crowds behind to get into unspoilt upland areas belonging to the Peak National Park. Definitely my sort of walking!

Down Cumberland Clough to Wildboarclough, Shutlingsloe in the distance

Walk: WB1

Wildboarclough, Gradbach and Three Shire Heads

Starting Point: Old quarry car park in Wildboarclough, 200m north of the Crag Inn – near a junction, and a sign to 'Buxton 6'. SJ983688.

How to get there: turn off the Macclesfield-Buxton Old Road at the Stanley Arms. Drive down the minor road for 2½ miles to a junction with bridge crossing river.

Map: OS Explorer OL 24 – The Peak District, White Peak Area

Length: 6½ miles

Grade: Moderate

Duration: Two and a half hours

Both Wildboarclough and Gradbach are pretty places to visit, while Three Shire Heads is ruggedly impressive and is also a very popular tourist spot – so, try to avoid summer weekends!

Head from the car park downhill for a few yards, then turn left over the bridge – noting the plaque commemorating the flood of 1989, which Laura, my elder daughter, and I well remember:

Aftermath of the 1989 flood in Wildboarclough: Laura in foreground!

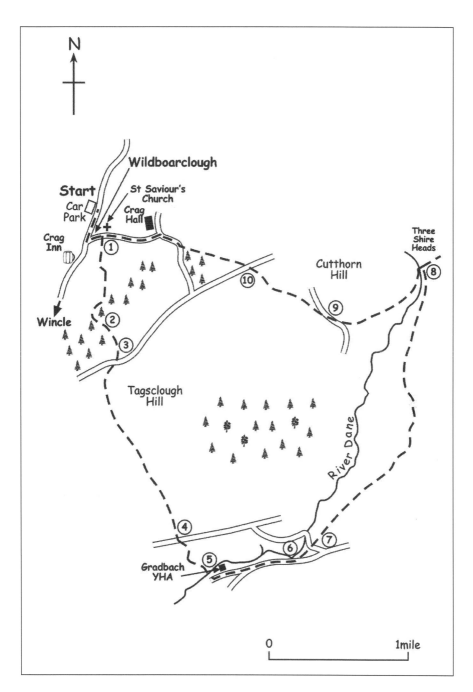

N

Wildboarclough

Start
Car
Park

St Saviour's
Church

Crag
Hall

Crag
Inn

①

Wincle

②

③

Tagsclough
Hill

Three
Shire
Heads

⑧

Cutthorn
Hill

⑨

⑩

River Dane

④

⑤

Gradbach
YHA

⑥

⑦

0   1mile

Pass the old post office (see introduction to this section) and take a right turn along a track (1) just after a telephone box on your left.

The path continues straight ahead after passing the house on your left. Walk alongside a dry-stone wall and then cross a stile. Continue through the field to the top-left-hand corner, where you turn left and walk between two stone walls. Then, go over a footbridge at the wall corner on your right and aim for the top-left-hand corner of the next field. From here, follow the obvious uphill track between a pair of stone walls.

At the end of this track (also at the farthest reach of the wood), turn left over a stone stile and go straight ahead, towards the next wood (2). Keep this wood on your right, then head for a stone-built building straight ahead. Walk through the farmyard of this old farm and follow the grassy track towards the road (3), heading towards a stepped stile some 40m to the left of a gate.

Cross the road, and the stile almost opposite, leading upwards to a tarmac track around the hill. At the first fork in this track, where the tarmac ends, keep left and follow a stony track all the way to the road. As you reach the highest point on this track, you may be able to see the sharp peaks of the Roaches straight ahead while a backward glance over your right shoulder should reveal Croker Hill with its communication tower – depending on the weather.

Cross the road (4) and follow the farm track as far as its sharp bend to the right, where you continue straight ahead, over a stile and onto a permissive path. Head downhill with the wall on your right, then turn left when you reach the wall facing you. Walk alongside the wall and turn right through a wide gap, where there once was a stile, and fork slightly left to join a track leading downhill to Gradbach Youth Hostel (5), originally a silk mill.

> It seems a shame that this, of all youth hostels, does not yet have a café on the premises – especially since the demise, due to EU bureaucracy, of the Eagle and Child café on the road above the hostel. The hostel once had a cold drinks machine – on a summer's day this was akin to a desert oasis, but the Peak District National Park didn't like it (Why? Wrong colour? Wrong drinks?) and enforced its removal. You can, however, now call into the hostel for drinks and chocolate bars – and there's a chance that a seasonal café may open. Unless, of course, the bureaucrats find out first.

From the hostel, follow the private drive to the left and uphill. At the end of the drive, turn left along a minor road. Some years ago, it was

The old post office, Wildboarclough

possible to follow a concessionary path parallel to the road, but it is mostly obstructed with vegetation and is impassable most of the time, even though it claims to be on the route of the Dane Valley Way (DVW). Therefore, walk along the road for about 250m, enter a car park and find the footpath in the far right-hand corner. Follow the footpath from here (DVW marker) along a riverside, then cross a footbridge (6) and follow the path alongside the River Dane on your left. Leave the field by a stile adjacent to a gateway and turn right.

Walk along the road for some 70m, then turn left (7) through a gateway with a public footpath sign. Pass Dane View House on your left and bear right, through a gateway and uphill through a small gate. From here, carry on straight ahead, with the wall on your left and enjoy a lengthy wallside walk for almost as far as the eye can see – no problems with navigation. Along the way, pass a large barn on your right and continue with distant buildings as a reference point.

After a second mini-gate, march up the final uphill stretch and, finally, you reach the very end of the wall. From here, continue in the same direction over two stiles. After the second stile, head for the top-left-hand corner of the field. Go through a gap then follow the wall on your left, crossing a hardcore track. Cross a stile into the next field then walk uphill and to the left of the derelict building facing you. Where the path joins a farm track which is walled on both sides, turn left and continue straight ahead – ignore any footpath signs, side tracks or paths: just follow the main track with the River Dane over to the left until you reach the bridges at Three Shire Heads (8). Cross both bridges and turn left so that you are again above the Dane. Continue along the track circling Cutthorn Hill until you reach the road.

Cross the road (9), then immediately go over a stile to the right of a house and follow the path. Initially, this runs alongside the wall, then gently forks right to continue straight ahead, wandering across open moorland that had been classified as an 'Environmentally Sensitive Area' before 'right to roam' legislation. Eventually, the path crosses a gap in a stone wall – some 30m to the right of where the wall crumbles into oblivion.

Shutlingsloe is a beautiful sight ahead, as the path curves very slightly to the right and leads to the main road – you'll see the footpath sign quite soon. Cross the road (10) and then the stile facing you. Continue along a well-maintained path, again towards Shutlingsloe. Where the path meets the road, turn right and follow the road downhill, passing to the left of Crag Hall (country seat of Lord Derby), St Saviour's church (where you can buy a booklet about Wildboarclough) and the old post office, back to the car park.

Walk: WB2
Wildboarclough, Shutlingsloe and Langley

Starting Point: Old quarry car park in Wildboarclough, 200m north of the Crag Inn – near a junction, and a sign to 'Buxton 6'. SJ983688.

How to get there: turn off the Macclesfield-Buxton Old Road at the Stanley Arms. Drive down the minor road for 2½ miles to a junction with bridge crossing river.

Map: OS Explorer OL 24 – The Peak District, White Peak Area

Length: 8 miles

Grade: Moderate/strenuous

Duration: 3½ hours

The only strenuous part of the walk is the ascent of Shutlingsloe – the prominent hill that you'll see from many walks in this book. Its ascent is justifiably popular and you'll rarely be up there alone, so perhaps a weekday visit would be better if you prefer your own company!

From the car park head downhill, following the Wincle/Congleton sign. In about 50m turn sharp right (1) up a private road (also a public path). As you pass the private drive to Bank Top, Shutlingsloe with a trig point on its right 'shoulder' becomes dramatically visible – and with quite a different flat-topped shape from its sharp-pointed aspect when viewed from the north.

At the last wall before Shutlingsloe Farm, turn left and follow the waymarked path steeply uphill to the summit. After this, the route is ahead and down a stone-slabbed track – but not before you've used the handy toposcope (plaque with surrounding points of interest) provided by the Peak & Northern Footpaths Society. After the descent and at the end of the flat section where the path meets a second one from the right, turn left (2) over a plank bridge, following the Peak and Northern sign to Langley. Eventually, you reach the outskirts of Macclesfield Forest. Cross the stile (3) into the forest and turn immediately left. Walk downhill, soon joining a wider track, and head towards Trentabank reservoir.

> As an aside, it used to be possible to cut the walk short by using the concessionary path that ran south from this path across High Moor; this is now closed, allegedly to protect threatened species.

Shutlingsloe from Wildboarclough

Ignore all side turns and, as you emerge from the densest part of the forest, turn left (4) along the gravel track signed to 'Trentabank & Gritstone Trail'. After a few hundred metres, turn left along a path marked with 'Langley via Gritstone Trail'.

Cross a wide forest track and continue along a grassy path signed 'To Gritstone Trail' until you join a minor road. Turn left and continue on this road for a short distance, then pass through an intriguing stile (designed, presumably, with pushchairs in mind) and go straight ahead on an aggregate track, all the way down to Ridgegate reservoir. At the bottom, there's a super view across the reservoir to the Leather's Smithy pub set invitingly below the rugged outline of Tegg's Nose – but disappointingly, we're not going there. Instead, follow the track alongside the reservoir and then head left (marked 'Forest Walk'). In less than 200m, turn left at the Gritstone Trail sign (5).

Go down some stone steps and over a bridge; turn right across a stile and then left to join a wide track heading towards a house. Keep to the right of the boundary fence, following the Gritstone Trail signs. The Trail is clearly waymarked and passes through a series of gates and pastures – just be sure to follow the directions of the waymarks, which I have found

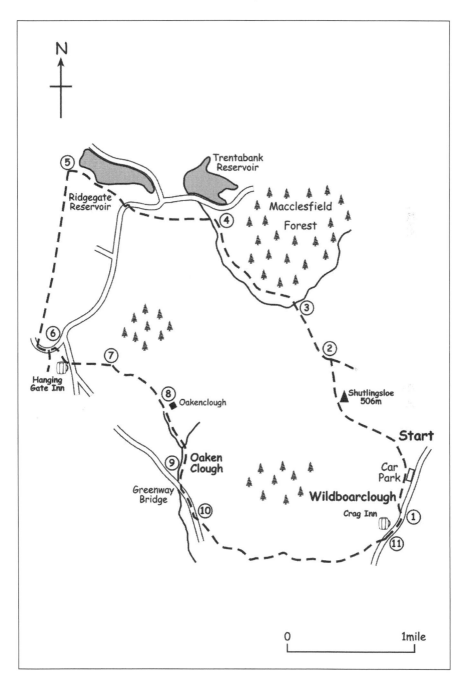

to be accurate. *(In case you'd like some reassurance, about a quarter of a mile after the house with the boundary fence, the Trail crosses a lane via two flights of steep steps. It passes a well-tended garden and alongside a line of conifers, then past a group of buildings. After a wooden stable, there's an uphill stretch without any waymarks so be sure to break through the line of trees that's facing you and head to a stile in the top-left corner.)*

After following waymarks for almost a mile, and soon after the stile mentioned in the previous sentence, farm buildings and a road are espied ahead. Keep to the left of the fencing, then cross a stile and turn left at the road to leave the Gritstone Trail. After 200m take the *second* footpath (6) on the right (i.e. *not* the one at the entrance to 'The Steps'). This path leads directly to the beer garden of The Hanging Gate – at an altitude of 1098ft, this 17th-century inn is noted both for its fine food and for one of the best views in Cheshire from its famous 'View Room'.

After a break, cross the road and the stile facing you, then walk uphill to another stile (7). Turn right here, then left through a gateway. Keep the wall on your left and continue to the corner of two stone walls where there is a waymark sign. This also marks the end-point of the now-defunct concessionary path across High Moor. From here, continue ahead (almost easterly) passing two small ponds. As the path goes over a hill, you'll see Oakenclough, the large property ahead.

The path descends towards a large pool below the house (8). Footpath purists may wish to use the right of way that goes straight ahead, uphill, and around the wall surrounding the house then back down into the valley. The rest of us can avoid the climb by keeping to the right of the pool and following the waymarked permissive path down Oaken Clough to the road, where you turn left (9).

Continue along the road and fork left at a footpath sign along a farm track (10). Where the track bends sharply to the left, leave the track and cross a stile on your right. Bear left to go through a gateway then fork right, heading between the second and third power-line poles from the left; and aiming towards a clear gap in a distant wall, though that is not your destination.

This well-used path contours below Shutlingsloe by crossing a stream then forking right towards a stile at the right-hand end of a stone wall. From here, continue straight ahead through a series of waymarked gates. Eventually, the Crag Inn comes into view and the path drops down to a final gate (11) where you turn left and return to the car park.

Walk: WB3
The Cat and Fiddle, Errwood and Burbage Edge

Starting Point: Lay-by near the Cat and Fiddle Inn, on the A537 (SK001719).

How to get there: too obvious to explain – but do not use the car park of the Cat and Fiddle (the second-highest pub in England), instead park in the large lay-by opposite to the pub or the roadside near the turn for Derbyshire Bridge, just a short distance away in the direction of Buxton.

Map: OS Explorer OL 24 – The Peak District, White Peak Area

Length: 9 miles or 12 miles

Grade: Moderate/strenuous

Duration: Four hours or six hours

As an 'East Cheshire Walk', this may seem like a bit of a cheat: it begins in Cheshire, but much is in Derbyshire and, if you opt for the longer walk, part is in Staffordshire! However, my defence is that it would be a shame not to include a walk in an area that can be so rugged and icy in the winter, a paradise in spring and summer – and yet so temptingly near. The views are amazing, and there's even some industrial archaeology included for the historians amongst you. And that's not all: time it right and you could be rewarded with a fabulous sunset followed by a pint at the second highest pub in England, or an excellent afternoon tea at the Peak View café to negate all the benefits of the walk!

If you plan to call at the Peak View, phone 01298 22103 to check that it's going to be open on the day of your walk.

From your chosen parking spot, head along the road in the direction of Macclesfield and turn right at the first footpath sign on your right, at a bend in the road (1). Continue on a track and, after about 300m, with the Peak View café tantalisingly ahead, fork right. After almost a kilometre, pass stiles with signs pointing (right) to Goytsclough quarry and go ahead through a kissing gate (2) to a signpost pointing left to Shining Tor (which you don't want) and to Errwood (which you do). Continue ahead and head downhill, enjoying the views of Errwood reservoir and the wild moors beyond. There really is a moor called Wild Moor across there!

About 15 minutes later, turn left (3) through a gate in the wall (signpost to Errwood Hall via Shooters Clough). Follow the swooping zigzags, cross a stream and continue on a path through the rhododendrons. Walk between stone walls to a T-junction and turn right (signpost to Errwood Hall). From here you can make a diversion up some steps to visit the burial ground; return the same way to rejoin the track. Continue along the main track, then fork left between large stone gateposts to the remains of the hall.

There used to be an explanatory board here, briefly describing the history of the hall and its owners, the Grimshawe family. The hall was demolished in the 1930s on health and safety grounds when the reservoirs were constructed — I have never been able to understand this act of vandalism. For further information on the family and the hall, visit www.grimshaworigin.org/Webpages2/ErrwoodGoyt.htm

After inspecting the remains, continue on the same track towards the top end of a small valley. Cross the stream via a planked bridge and, immediately after, at a T-junction, turn right. From here, go straight ahead to follow the 'woodland walk' sign. After a short climb, turn right at the next junction to head downhill to a road.

Turn left here and walk to the north end of the reservoir. Follow the road across the dam (4) then, after passing the WC block at Bunsal Cob, begin to climb steeply. To avoid a long slog on tarmac, about 200m later, just after a small plantation (5), turn left through a gate. The track leads straight ahead and continues until just before a steep drop, near a small rocky outcrop (6). Turn right here and continue uphill, eventually crossing a stile to the left of a gateway and reaching the road again (7).

Turn right here then, just after a car park and a pool on your left, turn left along the track of the former Cromford and High Peak railway, now a wheelchair-friendly route. Walk along the course of the track until 50m before the bricked-up tunnel entrance (8), where you turn left, with a signpost to 'Buxton and Bishops Lane'. Start by following the wall and, at the top, bear slightly right (9). Burbage Edge lies to the right.

Go straight ahead (houses on the outskirts of Buxton are in the distance) to a stile on the right of a wood. Cross the stile and follow the path downhill. Where the footpath meets the road, turn right (10) and walk for about 300m to a small lodge (11), where you turn right along the road past Plex Farm, leaving the lodge behind you. At the top of this road, turn left (12) to re-join the railway track-bed.

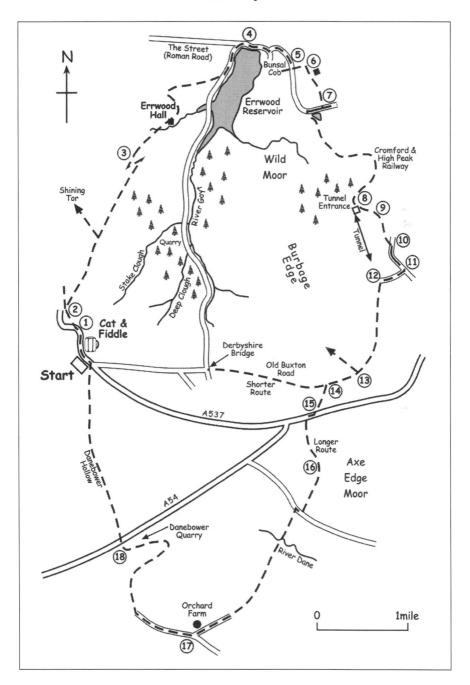

The former Cromford and High Peak railway

At the end of the line, bear right to join the old Buxton-Macclesfield turnpike – now just a rough track. After about 50m, there is a stile (13) and a signpost pointing right to 'Shining Tor and Lamaload' (13). This is a possible return route, leading across the River Goyt, then south of Shining Tor to the starting point.

If not taking this route, continue along the old turnpike. Ignore the first stile on your left, but continue for a further 200m to a stile with liftable dog gap (14). From here, there is another opportunity to cut the walk short: continue along the old turnpike and then, from the Derbyshire Bridge junction, walk up the tarmac road to your starting point – a total of 2½ miles that needs no further explanation.

Completing the Longer Walk

This includes an interesting visit to some old quarries, but there's a small section of tricky navigation that's made a whole lot easier with a compass. From the stile with the dog gap (14) referred to above, the path, level at first, slants gently away from the fence and crosses a stream before winding up a steep incline. Ignore the cattle track to the left – this is of no help; on your route, there is only a faint path and even that disappears as the gradient lessens. **The really important thing** is that you must stick to a south-west bearing across the side of the hill; do not be tempted to head for the highest point – just keep it on your right. Walk to the right of a minor ravine and then through an area of reeds until, if your navigation is correct, the land levels out at the second of two small pools. From here, the road is straight ahead, but you bear slightly right (SSW), now walking parallel to the main road on your left and towards a row of fenceposts on the skyline. After 100m, pass a rock-lined mineshaft – a reminder that this area was once the most important source of coal for Buxton and surroundings – and reach a wide, green track. Turn left here and walk along the track towards the road; cross a concrete slab over a culvert, then fork right towards a stile next to a gate (15). This track must surely have been connected with transport of coal from the mines.

Navigational note: The OS map shows a confusion of paths as you reach the main Buxton-Macclesfield road but, having walked and re-walked the first stretch several times, all I can say is that the above route is reliable. Even if you diverge slightly from the route, you are virtually certain to hit the broad green track and, so long as you remember to turn left, you will end up at the same place.

Cross the stile, turn right and, after 50m, cross the road and go over a stile to a clear track across Axe Edge Moor. Follow the track for a few minutes, passing another bricked-up mineshaft. The track bends left and, a little later, you turn right at a T-junction (16), before heading south to a minor road. Here, go right for a few paces then left along a signposted path. You soon cross the infant River Dane, then climb a minor slope. Cross a stile in the stone wall marking the Derbyshire/Staffordshire border and fork right. After a few minutes, turn right along a wide track and continue for about a kilometre (a slightly shorter route across boggy and tussocky moorland exists but is scarcely used). There is a ravine on the left and quarrying up to the right, the first intimation of the once-extensive quarrying and mining in the area.

Cross a stile just before the entrance to Orchard Farm and follow the track high above, and across, a stream. The track soon becomes a minor tarmac road and, after a very short distance, you take a fork to the right (17) passing a sign to Black Clough farm. (Note that the tarmac minor road extends for a great deal further than shown on some OS maps.) After about 100m the road re-crosses the stream, and there is a small parking area and a footpath sign (currently prostrate) for the Dane Valley Way (DVW). Fork right here and go uphill; walk past a 'Y' shaped stonewall structure, across a concrete track, and under telephone wires to a wide green track.

Turn left onto this track and contour around the hillside, keeping to the highest of the various tracks, to reach the head of the valley, where you turn sharp left and contour around the other side.

Continue for about a kilometre on a clear track to Reeve Edge quarries. Here, turn left between stone abutments (these may have enclosed a winding engine for the quarry) and pass a derelict building on the left. Continue to the head of this second valley, descend to cross the River Dane and follow DVW signs uphill along the main track through Danebower Quarries.

> Note: after heavy rain you may have to walk upstream to find a safe place to cross. Polly, my friend John's intrepid dog, was almost swept away here and then came near to drowning in a nearby pool just seconds later!

You soon reach a large chimney on your left (18), the most prominent relic of Danebower Colliery – for in the 18th and 19th centuries, this entire area was a scene of considerable industrial activity. Turn right from the chimney and climb steeply uphill to a footpath sign by the crash barrier. Cross the road here and follow the obvious track along Danebower Hollow – a lengthy moorland stretch with (on a clear day) glorious open views, all the way to the starting point at the Cat and Fiddle.

Back at the car

Whichever route you chose, it is worth pausing before driving away, as the views from here can be exceptionally photogenic. In March 1994, I returned at about half past six after an unseasonal fall of snow. I looked south-west, to the right of Shutlingsloe, and watched the biggest red ball of a sun I'd ever seen dipping behind the hills and reflecting off the snow. In November 2003 I was hurrying back after my first reconnoitre of the extension to the walk – anxious that I might have cut it too fine. But patches of brown heather were turned crimson by the setting sun – I was late, but not too late!

Whether or not you are as fortunate, you should still have enjoyed the walk. So, turn left and follow the track back to the road and your car. If there was no sunset, look on the bright side – the Cat and Fiddle should be open! Or, there's the excellent Peak View café just down the road.

WILMSLOW

This section is the largest in the book, in terms of the total number of walks. This is partly due to it being my 'local patch', but is also because it includes parts of Styal, Chorley, Great Warford and Mobberley. The walks themselves all begin in Wilmslow, before straying over the boundaries.

Wilmslow, like Alderley Edge, is very much a railway town in that the railway companies offered incentives to house builders in the shape of cut-price tickets to Manchester. Because of this, there are those who argue that Wilmslow has no history but, just to prove them wrong, there is the little matter of 'Lindow Man'. This well-preserved body was discovered in the peat deposits near to Lindow Common.

St Bartholomew's, Wilmslow

The peat of Lindow has been a small local industry for many years. Some peat is still cut, but in a 1935 edition of *Cheshire Life* it was reported that thousands of pieces of peat were cut every day. The work must have been hard, for each worker alone was said to cut around 1000 pieces per day – indicating that the workforce must have been fairly small. Most of the peat was used for fire-lighters, after being soaked in creosote. Nowadays, it is mainly used for mushroom cultivation. There are all sorts of rumours as to what it may become in the future!

The two main park

areas of Wilmslow are The Carrs recreation area and Lindow Common. The latter is a Site of Special Scientific Interest (SSSI) and its main feature is Black Lake, the attraction of which is marred only by an ugly wire fence.

The name 'Wilmslow' derives from the Anglo-Saxon for 'William's Mound' and then, as now, the surrounding land must have been primarily agricultural. Since then there have been other industries, notably the silk and cotton mills dotted around the area. Wilmslow's own silk mill operated until 1923, when it burnt down – due, it was thought, to the unsafe storage of gelatine. Quarry Bank Mill at nearby Styal was of far greater importance; it was developed in various stages by the Greg family from 1787 to 1939, when it was handed over to the National Trust. The mill lies at the centre of Styal Country Park and is of interest not only as a restored cotton mill, but also as the hub of a self-contained village. You can still see the mill workers' houses and visit the chapel, school and apprentice house.

The mill lies on the River Bollin which, despite local folklore, has no provable connection with Anne Boleyn. But the Bollin is very influential on the area both in terms of motive power for the old mills, and for its effect on the landscape as it meanders along the wide area of the Bollin Valley. Slowly, it is being cleaned up as less effluents are dumped into it upstream.

The Walks

This is rich agricultural land with no high hills to climb. The walks are all 'easy' but varied, both in their connections with local history, and the variations in terrain. The land is gently undulating, being at its best around the Bollin.

Walk: W1

A Walk Around the Bollin

Starting Point: Twinnies Bridge car park, Wilmslow, at the western end of The Carrs, SJ839823.

How to get there: the only entrance to the car park is from the B5166 Styal Road (see map), part-way from Wilmslow to Styal.

Map: OS Explorer 268 – Wilmslow, Macclesfield & Congleton

Length: 5 miles (or 3½ miles).

Grade: Easy

Duration: two and a half hours (or two hours)

The River Bollin is your constant companion for most of this walk and there's plenty to see along the way, including Styal Mill and the varied woodland, birdlife and rolling rural landscape that surround Wilmslow. This is pretty much unchanged since the first (1985) edition of my 'East Cheshire Walks' – but in more recent editions I altered the route through Styal's Northern Woods so that you can see the attractive old bridges built for the mill owners.

From Twinnies Bridge car park (1) walk between the toilet block and the River Bollin to the bridge across the River Dean. Head for Quarry Bank Mill and **either** go straight ahead to keep close to the river (2) **or** cross Worm's Hill (to the right and uphill), along the path used by the mill apprentices for their Sunday treks to and from Wilmslow's parish church.

When you reach the mill, note the mill yard. The cobbles are 'erratics' – stones displaced from their usual locations by glacial action. Workers were paid to collect them during the 'Cotton Famine' of the early 1860s when supplies of cotton had dwindled due to the American Civil War and cotton spinning had been suspended.

The mill, together with the 500-acre Styal estate, was given to the National Trust by the Greg family in 1959. Live demonstrations and hands-on displays, combined with a magnificent 50-ton restored waterwheel and noisy, working cotton machinery recreate the spirit of the Industrial Revolution. The mill is open from 11am to 5pm every day in the

Styal Mill: the clock and bell ensured strict timekeeping for the employees

summer and from 11am to 4pm, Wednesday to Sunday, in the winter. The garden of Quarry Bank House first opened its gates to the public in 2008. For current hours phone 01625 527468 or visit the website at tinyurl.com/a3pz44.

Carry on past the mill and up the tarmac drive. Along the way, look out for a cobbled footpath, signposted to Morley, on the left. This was part of a packhorse route from Northwich to Yorkshire, used for the transport of salt in one direction, and wool on the return journey. A particular advantage for the packhorse masters ('jaggers') was that it avoided crossing the Lancashire boundary and thereby escaped two sets of tolls. Nowadays, you can use it as a short cut – see note at end of the walk description.

Pass Quarry Bank House and continue uphill, noticing the occasional large cobblestones set into the side of the drive: these enabled horse-drawn carts to pause for a while, so that the horses could have a breather. 100m or so up the drive, turn left (3) as indicated by the 'Northern Woods' sign and turn sharp, hairpin left at the National Trust sign ('Styal – To the Woods') along a footpath that leads above Quarry Bank House.

Pass the entrance to Norcliffe Gardens and, with a wood to your left and a field to your right, proceed to a T-junction with a notice board. Turn right here, then left across the arched wooden bridge. Turn left again and follow the path which soon zigzags down stone steps and crosses Chapel Bridge, constructed for Robert Greg as a convenient route to the mill from nearby Norcliffe Hall. Having crossed the bridge, keep left again on a path with a steep ravine on your left and go generally downhill, above the lovely stone-arched Folly Bridge, all the way to Kingfisher Bridge (but there's no guarantee of seeing a kingfisher!).

Don't cross this bridge but instead turn right, following the Bollin downstream and continuing on a wide, obvious track – keep left at a fork in the path to stay alongside the Bollin. The river is getting cleaner nowadays with fish and wildfowl along its entire length; chub, dace and trout are increasingly common. The next bridge is Oxbow Bridge (4) – oxbow lakes are created by the constant erosion of soft riverbanks by a meandering river such as the Bollin. There's no oxbow lake here as yet and you'd have to wait many years for one to form, so cross the bridge and turn left (upstream for a short distance), then up and down flights of steps to reach the river again. Follow the path to 'Giant's Castle Bridge'

(5), largely paid for by the proceeds of a sponsored walk from Land's End to John O'Groats some years ago. Note the brick arch in the far bank of the river: this is the end of the tailrace tunnel from Styal Mill, some three-quarters of a mile upstream from here.

Cross the bridge then climb 135 steps to the rocky outcrop of Giant's Castle. Not sure about the 135? Run back down and count them again! Continue and descend 92 steps (how odd!) and follow the path between the river and the woods, all the way to the 'old' road leading to the Holiday Inn hotel (6).

Immediately before the car park of the hotel, turn right along a narrow snicket, keeping the high wooden fence on your left. If the snicket is too overgrown, walk through the hotel car park instead. Either way, emerge onto the pavement and cross the busy A538 to a kissing gate and signpost to the right of a bus stop. The path goes across the field with the river far to your right, through another gate and then up a steep slope and almost straight across a large field. Bear slightly left and cross a footbridge, then turn left to follow the field edge. This leads to a stile with a Bollin Valley Way marker and then towards the hamlet of Shady Grove. Continue along a track, past a house with yapping dogs, to Dooleys Lane and then on to Morley Green Road. Turn left here for 250m and then right at a tarmac drive (7) with signpost.

Continue along the drive on what soon becomes a cobbled surface, and pass some handsome white-painted cottages. Keep to the right of a garage, cross a stile and follow a waymark (45 degrees left) across the field to the next stile. Go straight ahead to another stile leading onto a country lane (8). Turn right here and continue for about 200m to Moss Grove Farm (9) where you turn left and follow an ancient green lane to Mobberley Road. Turn left here and walk to the A538, which you cross to join a track.

Shortly before a bridge (10), turn left (Bollin Valley Way sign) and follow the pleasant path through the woods behind King's Road and Wilmslow Rugby Club. This stretch is a delight in springtime, with wonderful displays of bluebells on the banks and Pigginshawe Brook far below How can such a small stream have cut such a deep ravine?

There's a helpful stretch of boardwalk through a particularly damp area (lots of water-loving wild flowers to identify) before you re-join the Bollin. Very soon, you cross the bridge over the river and you're back at Twinnies car park.

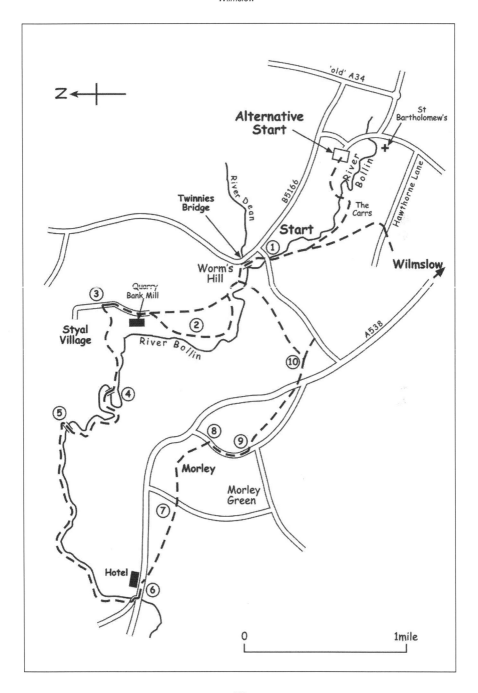

Notes

Alternative start: you can start from the Parish Hall at the other end of The Carrs, but note that the car park is now pay-and-display with a two-hour limit except on Sundays. From here take either the dog-walkers' route alongside the river, or the less-well-used public path through the wooded slope on your extreme left of The Carrs. This latter path leads you below the ruins of the private chapel of Pownall Hall (St Olaf's), then drops down to Twinnies car park.

Short cut: to cut a mile and a half off the route, after walking through the mill yard at Styal Mill, turn left at the cobbled footpath, signposted to Morley. Follow this up to a farm and go through its often muddy farmyard to the A538. Turn right, pass the Honey Bee pub then take the first turn left towards Morley Green. Follow the rest of the walk from point (7), having turned left along the tarmac drive.

Walk: W2

Wilmslow to Mottram Bridge

Starting Point: Car Park, Wilmslow Parish Hall/Carrs Recreation area, SJ848815.

How to get there: find the church, and you've found the car park!

Map: OS Explorer 268 – Wilmslow, Macclesfield & Congleton

Length: 5 miles

Grade: Easy

Duration: Two and a half hours

Leave the car park and turn right along Chancel Lane, passing the Parish Church and then the Garden of Remembrance. Turn left (Bollin Valley sign) and walk along Mill Street. Cross Manchester Road to the left of the roundabout and continue along the A538 by-pass feeder. Before the next roundabout (1), bear left and then head right, through the underpass. Follow the River Bollin upstream to Bollin Bridge (2) where you turn right and walk through part of the Wilmslow Park development towards Macclesfield Road. Cross the road, and join a tarmac road (almost opposite) leading to Queen Anne Court. After 50m, keep left along a tarmac path to the left of wooden fencing. Continue to Land Lane and walk through a housing estate built on the grounds of the former Thorngrove site of Wilmslow High School (3).

Walk along Land Lane and go over an embankment, by way of a double flight of steps, to the Prestbury link road. Cross this busy road, turn left and walk a few metres to a footpath sign and the remains of a kissing gate.

This is where the 'real' walk begins. Continue along a well-trodden footpath for almost 150m, passing allotments on the right. You come to the corner of a large uncultivated field – actually several fields ploughed into one, so the old field boundaries are obliterated. The right of way crosses the field, as waymarked, almost diagonally – **not** around the edge! Walk due south, heading for a wooded dip.

When you get to the dip, walk across as waymarked then bear right to a hedge corner. Follow the next waymark and a white house comes into

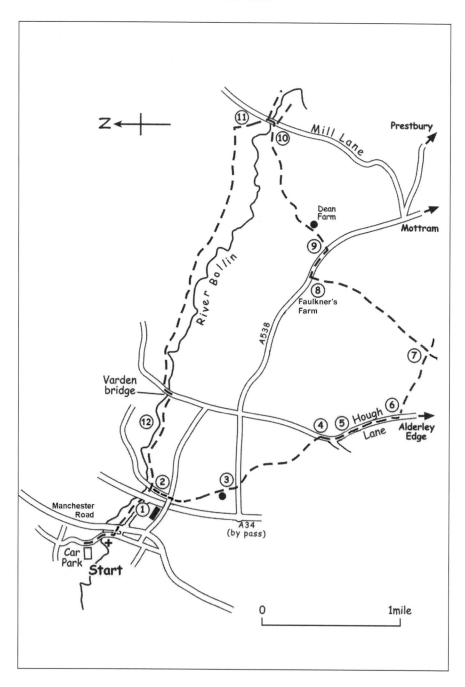

view in the distance. Head towards this and find a stile in the far corner of the field. Cross the stile and go through a wood, following the waymarks. The footpath emerges at Hough Lane (4), where you turn right and then bear left at the fork, soon passing Chonar Farmhouse (5) and Hough Green Farm – which may become 'footballer mansions' to judge from nearby developments!

Continue along Hough Lane for another 50m and turn left at a stile alongside a gate (6). Follow the hedge on your left and, after passing some mature trees, cross a stile (7) in the hedge (NCW sign) then turn right and continue, with the hedge on your right, in the same direction to a footpath sign. Turn left here (do not cross the stile) and follow the hedge on your right along the entire length of this big field. At the far right corner, cross a stile and continue with the hedge now on your left. Cross another stile and then, after 50m or so, turn left across a footbridge and follow the waymark.

Pass under power lines and go over a stile in the corner of a field. Follow the waymarks from here, heading just to the right of the Faulkner's Farm development (8). Two waymarked kissing gates lead you to the A538 (Prestbury Road) (8). Turn right and walk for 200m along this busy main road; **take care: walk on the verge and face oncoming traffic; cross to the left-hand side for the final 100m.**

Turn left at the impressive poplar-lined drive (9) to Dean Farm. Go past the buildings, then through a gateway and follow the waymark signs downhill with a large fence on the right. At the next gate, continue alongside the fence and cross a ladder stile into a small wood. Go over a footbridge and turn right towards a stile. Cross this and turn left, with the hedge on your left. Continue for 100m to a break in the hedge and bear right as waymarked. Pass or cross a stile in a wire fence, and you reach Mill Lane by way of a stile about 10 metres left of a gate. Here, turn left, cross Mottram Bridge (10) and turn left (11) to head back to Wilmslow along the well-maintained and waymarked Bollin Valley Way, with the River Bollin away to your left.

Very soon, the path climbs a grassy bank to the right, heading towards houses. From here, look back to the meandering Bollin and its wide flood plain. Winter floods cause rapid erosion of the sandy banks; the landscape responds more rapidly to dramatic events than to gentle persuasion.

Just before the houses, go through a kissing gate and turn left – spot the weather vane on the garage in the shape of a racing car! Follow the

The weir on the River Bollin

waymarks until you reach a three-armed signpost. Turn left here (tempting as it is, do **not** cross the stile) then right at the next stile to follow the Bollin. Cross Varden Bridge at the main road and soon you will hear – and then see – the impressive weir (12) in the Bollin.

This was used to control the water level to a silk mill, which closed in 1923. Look carefully on your left and you'll find the remains of the mill race below the houses in Macclesfield Road. The weir was repaired in 2004 and it was intended to have had a salmon ladder, in anticipation of further improvements downstream. That's been delayed, but fishing in the cleaned-up River Bollin is already a popular – though not strictly legal – pastime. Trout have been seen both above and below the weir.

Cross the next road and retrace your steps to the start of the walk.

Walk: W3
Wilmslow to Castle Hill, via Runway 2

Starting Point: Car park in Racecourse Road, SJ833814

How to get there: off the A538 near the Boddington Arms. Use this only as a starting or meeting point; cars parked here are a prime target for thieves and vandals – park on a side road instead.

Map: OS Explorer 268 – Wilmslow, Macclesfield & Congleton

Length: 10 miles (or 6 miles using short cut)

Grade: Easy/ Moderate

Duration: Five hours (an hour less with short cut)

Forget about bird-spotting or wildflowers – on this walk, you'll need a spotter's guide to aircraft, because you'll be walking around and under the runways of Manchester International Airport. Because of the building of Runway 2, the walk in earlier editions of this book has been changed very extensively, but it is probably more interesting than before. One feature remains the same: the large number of stiles. There were over 30, but by now there could be more! Note that if you go in the wintertime, or any time after prolonged rain, some stretches can be a bit muddy – not that mud deters dedicated plane spotters or stile connoisseurs!

Walk down the lane, then continue on a grassy track (follow footpath sign) and go over a stile. From here, bear right towards the far corner of the field, ignoring the stile on your right but following the two-way footpath sign perched in the middle of the field. Cross a stile and go over a small bridge, soon following a path through the woods and above the Bollin.

When you emerge from the trees and the path levels out, you come to a signpost (4) with three blank arms (very odd!) where you turn right through a gate. Pass through a second gate with the runway tunnel temptingly ahead – but bear left from here and soon slant uphill on the same bearing, then follow the fence around the copse on your right. Ignore any stiles – these are nothing to do with the main route – just keep going until you reach a third gate. Here, turn right towards the tunnel

1954: A Douglas Dakota IV crossing Yewtree Lane, then the main Wilmslow-Altrincham road. A watchman was employed to stop traffic. *(Photograph by A.M.G Armstrong)*

again and drop down towards an excellent interpretation panel which includes information on a nearby prehistoric settlement dating from the Neolithic/Early Bronze Age; this is part of the Runway Two Trail published by Manchester Airport and is downloadable as a PDF from: http://tinyurl.com/2wshued.

Cross the footbridge (5) over the River Bollin, turn left and walk through the bright and airy tunnel. Surprisingly, there is no barrier between the walkway and the river, so keep an eye on any children in your party. Emerge from the tunnel, pause to read the panel about the ecology of the immediate area, then turn left at a T-junction and follow the road. After 300m or so, turn left over a bridge and continue uphill as far as a cattle grid (6).

For a possible short cut: continue straight ahead across the cattle grid with the ILS (Instrument Landing System) area on your right, then pass a series of pools on your left until you reach point (10) – see map and instructions below; this cuts about 3 miles off the walk.

An Airbus A330-200 on Runway 2. The diverted River Bollin flows through the cathedral-like tunnel and the walkway is on the far side.

If continuing on the complete walk: turn right before the cattle grid (BVW sign) and walk along a wide gravel track. Very soon, you look down the entire length of Runway 1 is on your right. Begin circling to the left, keeping a hedge on your left. The route has stiles and waymark signs. On your left is the ILS area beyond the end of Runway 1.

Soon, you reach a pair of stiles, one ahead and one to the right. Cross the one to the right (BVW) and continue straight ahead from here, with a hedge on your right and a pond on the left. After a while, the path continues alongside a hedge and eventually reaches the access drive for Castle Hill Farm (7).

Turn left at the drive and, almost immediately, left again over a stile and into a field (if there's no electric fence dividing the field, just take a right-angle left without going onto the farm drive). Bear slightly right and head to a stile to the right of a tree; cross the stile and walk past a wooded pool on your right; the next stile is in the far left-hand corner, to the right of a pylon. Cross the stile and continue alongside a hedge, passing a stile and footpath sign. At the end of this field, cross a stile or go through the gateway, with a waymark pointing almost straight ahead towards yet another stile midway along the hedge, by a large tree and a small pool (8).

From here, the path bends to the left, passing left of a large pool, to another stile. Cross the next field to a signpost (9) and stile; cross this then turn left and begin walking through a series of gates and stiles, with Stock-in-Hey Farm eventually off to the left. Keep walking in the same (almost easterly) direction, across yet more stiles and watching for waymarks as the path jiggles about. Along the way, minor diversions take you past pools that have replaced ones lost in the construction of Runway 2. Eventually you reach a tarmac lane to start a lengthy loop around the end of the runway, soon glimpsed over to the left.

Now for a tour of the crash gates – necessary for emergency access to the airport: continue around the runway (10), soon passing Crash Gate 11, after which you go straight ahead along a signposted track. After crossing the access road to Crash Gate 10, follow the bridleway past the far end of the runway, soon passing a large pond on the left and going through a gateway. Turn left ('Runway 2 Trail' waymark), walk along a tarmac lane and pass through a gate towards Crash Gate 9. Walk along the bridleway, ignoring a signpost to the right but passing buildings on the right. Note Crash Gate 8 on your left, then fork left off the tarmac through a kissing gate and along a public footpath (11), with a fine stand of bulrushes on the right. Go through a gate and continue with a fence on your left, with yet more bulrushes over to the left.

With your mind now on less scary matters than plane crashes, go through the next gate, over a footbridge and turn right. Cross a stile and turn left along the road (Woodend Lane). After 30m, turn right (12) towards Oak Farm, keeping the fence on your right. Use the electricity post in the middle of the second field as a sight line to guide you to the footpath and stile to the right of the farm.

A few years ago, there was a seemingly docile bull in this field; a herd of bullocks led the bull towards our party, the bull became excited and he and his entourage chased me into a water-filled ditch, from which I ignominiously scrambled into the next field. The farmer may have had the law on his side, but it was bound to be a likely occurrence. My advice? If you see a bull, keep to the edge of the field and to hell with the right of way!

Cross the stile, turn left onto a road and then right into the farm. The path passes to the right of the farm buildings. Go across a series of waymarked stiles, then follow the line of the hedge, alternating from left to right and back to left again, **Note: watch out for the final left turn that takes you to the left-hand side of the hedge. This turn is very easy to**

Wilmslow

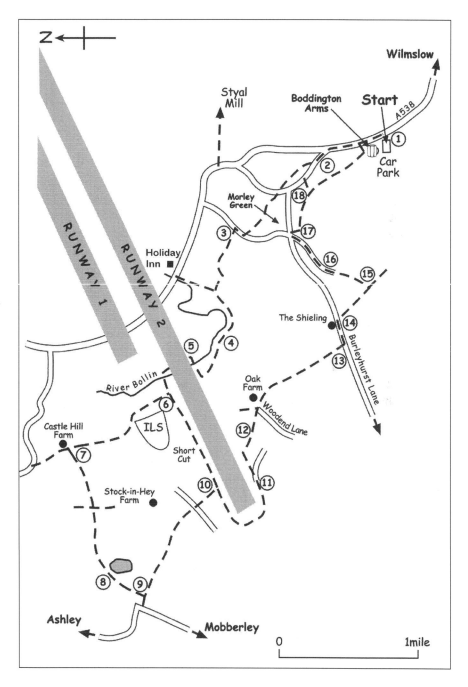

miss – in which case, you'll end up on the wrong side of the hedge! You eventually emerge at the road (13). Turn left here and walk past Burleyhurst Farm, with its magnificent Monkey Puzzle Tree. A strange tree – first found in about 1780 in Chile, where monkeys are not native but the tree is sacred to the indigenous Mapuche people.

Turn right just before the landmark tree, go over a stile and into the remains of a tree nursery (14). Keep ahead and slightly left, then cross a stile by a gate and continue on a raised track, passing a sign (partly hidden in the trees) pointing to the right. Ahead is an old stile (15) leading to a lake. Turn left here along an ancient tree-lined track, past the mobile home park on the right and through a gap in the trees with a wooden gatepost embedded in the undergrowth. From here, the path bears slightly right, over a small rise and past more mobile homes on your right to a further stile in the top-right-hand corner of the field. Go through this and then turn left to walk along Eccups Lane (16) to Mobberley Road.

Turn right here, then right again along a track opposite to Morley Green Road. **Note:** The Cheshire Smokehouse is a short diversion along Morley Green Road. Maybe the restaurant isn't ideal for sweaty and/or muddy walkers, but their pork pies and other products are highly recommended for picnics!

After a couple of minutes along the track, turn left at the first house ('Sunnyside') and continue (17) along a wide path. After about 400 metres, where the path bends left, turn right at a waymark through a gate on your right (18) and then go straight ahead with the hedge on your right until you reach a surfaced lane, Greaves Road. Follow this to Altrincham Road, where you turn right and return to the starting point.

Walk: W4
Wilmslow and Great Warford

Starting Point: Plough and Flail, SJ818798

How to get there: not the easiest of places to find. Drive along the B5085 Alderley Edge/Knutsford road and find Paddock Hill Lane, opposite to the road signed to Wilmslow Golf Club. Signs lead to the pub.

Map: OS Explorer 268 – Wilmslow, Macclesfield & Congleton

Length: 6 miles

Grade: Easy

Duration: Two and a half hours

Here's a classic pub walk, starting from the Plough and Flail in rural Cheshire – little more than a mile or so from the bustling centre of Wilmslow. Seldom-used footpaths take you to the outskirts of Alderley Edge, across to Great Warford and back along some quiet byways. There are absolutely no hills to climb and you should be able to complete the 6 miles in about two and a half hours.

The Plough & Flail: tucked away on a country lane

An inquisitive local at the start of the walk

Park near to the pub or ask permission if you wish to use the car park in anticipation of slaking your thirst on your return. Be sure to admire the handsome alpacas, resident here since 1994! Turn left out of the car park and walk along the road to a private drive on the right (1). The path goes to the left of the drive. Climb over two stiles and go through the next field to a collection of buildings (2). Pass in front of the buildings, go over a drive and through the gate to follow a path that soon becomes a track.

The track bends to the right and passes through a wooded area to a stile. Go over this and follow the left-hand edge of the wood facing you. Cross the next stile and soon you follow a clear path with trees either side. The paths around here are based on the Lindow Moss peat deposits.

A little way from here, 'Lindow Pete' was excavated in 1984. The body was remarkably well preserved and evidence suggests that he was the subject of a ritual execution. Alderley Edge lies ahead and, from time to time you will see the spire of the parish church, St Philip's.

The path eventually becomes a minor road and emerges at the B5085 (3). Turn right here, cross the road, then turn left down Carr Lane. Keep walking along the lane, soon passing the water treatment works and then Oak Ridge Farm, on your left. Continue ahead on a wide access drive until you reach a T-junction (large property with high wooden gates ahead). Turn right here and follow the clearly waymarked track – do not attempt to follow the path shown on OS maps to the east of the track, as it leads to the bypass! The main track leads to the A535 (4) which you cross (care!) and turn left, leading you safely **above** the bypass.

You are now on the outskirts of Alderley Edge. Continue in this direction for just over 200m and take the first turn right along Chorley Hall Lane, catching glimpses of Chorley Old Hall on your right. Turn right at the footpath sign along Green Lane, opposite to Windermere Drive. Follow the lane – more of a track – to a minor road, keep right, then almost immediately join another track. Keep walking for 10 minutes and,

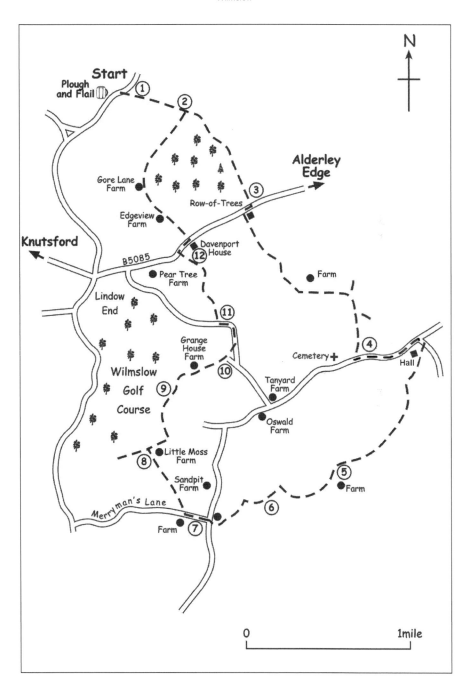

at the private drive to Field's Farm, a footpath continues behind a conifer hedge and then behind several large greenhouses (5). Keep the hawthorne hedge on your right and carry straight on.

Cross the next stile and, after a few metres, meet a fence with a stile set in it. Do not cross this; instead, keep left and follow the fence on your right all around the edge of the field. Along the way, cross two stiles, pass under electricity cables and you come to a pair of stiles and footbridge.

Cross these, turn left and cross another footbridge (6) over a drainage ditch. Bear slightly left, cross a stile, and then bear right towards a house. Cross the drive to the house and then bear left, following waymarks on the two large trees that lie ahead. Cross the next stile by the road sign to Alderley Edge.

Cross the A535 and continue along Merryman's Lane. After a couple of hundred metres or so, turn right at the footpath sign (7) just before a house. The path runs alongside a hedge and carries straight on, over a stile and then a gate. After the gate, walk alongside the edge of a large field to a signposted crossroads of paths. Cross the stile, turn right, and head towards Little Moss Farm (8). Turn left at the end of the fence before the farm and continue along a track, keeping the fence on your right until you cross a stream in the right-hand corner of the field. Cross a stile to enter another large field.

Despite the waymark directing you to the edge, the right of way goes straight across the field, first passing a pond on your right and then bearing left to a correctly waymarked stile. Go over this and then continue past Grange House Farm (9) and Willow Tree Farm. Immediately after Willow Tree Farm, the track bends to the right but there is a stile on the left. Hop over this, cross the next stile and continue to another stile near Orrells Well Farm (10).

Cross the stile, turn left and walk along the road (Foden Lane). Go over Foden Bridge and then turn right onto a path immediately after you have passed below the electricity cables (11). Head straight across the field to the hedge facing you. When you reach the hedge, turn left and follow it around to a stile, just after the point at which the hedge turns right. Now, follow the stiles to the B5085.

Turn right at the road, then left along Gore Lane (12). At the end of the lane – half a mile or so – there is a stile between two houses. Cross this, then three more stiles, and then carry on for 150m until you are back at location (2), the collection of buildings. Turn left here, and you're back at the Plough and Flail!

Walk: W5

Lindow, Saltersley and Mobberley

Starting point: Car park in Racecourse Road, SJ833814

How to get there: off the A538 near the Boddington Arms. See Walk W3.

Map: OS Explorer 268 – Wilmslow, Macclesfield & Congleton

Length: 9 miles

Grade: Easy

Duration: Four hours

This is an 'easy' but lengthy walk. Although it goes along some familiar routes, some little-used footpaths are included, which I feel are important in our local path network – especially when you need to plan circular walks like this one. Note: many paths cross this area and a 1:25000 OS map will be useful – be warned!

Start at the car park in Racecourse Road, opposite the Boddington Arms (1). Use this only as a starting or meeting point; do not park your car here: the car park is a prime target for thieves and vandals. Side roads tend to be a better choice, or maybe you can negotiate to use the pub car park.

Follow Racecourse Road to Lindow Lane (2), or cross Lindow Common if you know the paths. Go down the lane for a short distance and turn left at a bridleway (signed, but sometimes obscured by branches) along the drive to the first house on the left ('Bramford'). The path continues through a gate to the right of the house, then turns right and eventually joins another path at a T-junction (3). Cross a barrier and go straight ahead to meet a broad track. Turn left (4) past some makeshift stables. Go past a track that comes in from the left and turn right at the next T-junction (5). This path takes you past peat workings – some peat recovery still takes place, though there have been murmurings about a housing development or a nature reserve; we'll see.

When you reach a cross roads (6), you are at the westerly end of Newgate. If you've had enough, or the weather turns foul, you can turn right here and head back up Newgate to Lindow Common; there is a new path on the left (just past the entrance to the old waste disposal site)

which leads around the back of the old landfill site – it's much better than walking all along the road.

If continuing the walk, turn left and pass a bungalow on your right. A farm track goes towards a lake – actually the remains of a flooded sandpit. As the track bends left, you will see a stile. Although you *could* continue on the stony track, on this outward stretch of the walk, I'll take you to the right of the lake.

That's because the original right of way had been flooded and lost due to the new lake. Claiming this path took seven years of my life – doing battle with a laggardly Cheshire County Council and the local landowner to regain this right of way for you! So, cross the stile – having said "Thanks, Graham" – and follow the way-marked path.

The author leading intrepid walkers along a wetter-than-usual path

Towards the end of the lake, walk past a stile on the right and continue to the top of a slope. Turn left towards an overgrown hedge, then left again. Keep close to the hedge and emerge at a stile and signpost, where you turn right along the track. For a short walk, you could simply go all the way around the lake and then head for home. Please try this sometime: it really is very pleasant!

Having regained the track, ignore the first stile on your left, but carry on past Saltersley Hall Farm, joining the main farm drive. Turn left at the next stile (7) about 100m after the farm, and go straight across the field to a stile by a gate.

Parts of the farm are said to be more than 500 years old and to have been built with the same type of stone as used for Mobberley church. The expense of a stone-built dwelling indicates that this must have been an important building in its time – almost certainly because it was on the salt route (hence its name) from Northwich to Yorkshire, and it may well have provided accommodation for the jaggers (see page 104).

From here, the path continues ahead with the hedge on your left for the first few metres. Still on the same bearing, but moving slightly away from the hedge, head to the large single oak tree, and then straight ahead to the middle of the wooded area.

Find the stile in the corner of the field, to the left of the wooden fence of 'Hollingee' – the large property beyond the fence. Cross the stile and follow the waymark to the right. After 100m, turn left, soon passing the second tee of Styal Golf Course. Keep the hedge on your right and continue to Coppock House Farm (8). The path goes around the farm to join the farm drive. About 50m past the end of the drive, there is a stile (9) which will take you back to the Plough and Flail if you wish to shorten the walk. Otherwise, carry on past a bridleway on your right that would take you to the Quaker graveyard (a very worthwhile diversion) and past a group of houses.

Pass Egerton's repair shop, and keep walking along the road to its junction with Paddock Hill Lane (10). Turn right here. After 250m, you'll see a stile on the left, opposite to stables. Ignore this and continue for 100m until you reach a tiny bungalow on the left, called 'Pluto Cottage'; the stile you need is just before the cottage and is hidden behind a hedge (11). Find it, cross it and continue with the hedge on your right. Follow the stiles and waymarks until you reach the main Alderley-Knutsford road.

Cross the road and go slightly left of Sunny Bank Farm and follow the waymark to walk through the left-hand part of a barn (12). Bizarre, I know, but the route of this right of way was disputed for years and this is the result. Continue from the barn and along a broad track to a stile.

Cross the stile, and continue to a pair of stiles, from where you can see the Frozen Mop pub across the fields. From the second stile, head to the top-right-hand corner of the field and over a footbridge to yet another stile. Cross this, and continue to the road (13). Turn left here, go over Antrobus Bridge, then turn right up a drive. Just before a house with large iron gates, turn right through first one kissing gate and then a second. Follow the waymarked route between a fence and a hedge until, at the end of the hedge on your left, there is a stile. Cross this and continue in the same direction that you were walking, towards Coppock House, nestling in the woodland. To find the next stile, follow the fence to the corner of the field; turn left, then after 50m, you'll see a stile and a footbridge. Pass behind Coppock House (14) and walk through a parking area to a stile by a gate.

Continue straight ahead, until you reach a stile in a dip. From here, cross the next field by heading slightly to the right, towards a footpath sign. The stile is by the gate – cross this and carry on past Dam Head Farm (15) to the road, where you turn right from Damson Lane along Mill Lane

Dam Head Farm is appropriately named: there was a lake, and a dam, but no longer. But in Damson Lane, there are still damson trees! In Mill Lane, there's no longer a mill, but a choice of two pubs: The Bull's Head with its bowling green and the the more up-market Roebuck, a little further back.

Where Mill Lane joins the main road, cross over to the tarmac pavement and turn right. At the next road turn left along Church Lane. The footpath is now on the right, opposite to Gorsey Brow (16). Clamber over the stile, then cross the field diagonally, to the gate in the top-right-hand corner. Cross the next field and make for the kissing gate near the far right-hand corner. From here, there is a maze of paths and, to make things worse, there are small discrepancies between the paths as shown on the map and as they exist on the ground – so you'll need to follow these directions very carefully:

Cross the next field, again diagonally, to a kissing gate set in the fence about 100m short of the far corner. Continue to a sign and gate to the left of a farm (17). There is a junction of paths here, where you go ahead and slightly left to the next stile.

Cross the stile, bear right across the field then cross the next stile and keep the hedge on your left for a short distance. After the stile, continue in the same direction with a fence on your right – note that this boundary is not on OS maps. Continue in the same direction that you were previously walking, passing a single oak tree in the next field and then crossing a stile.

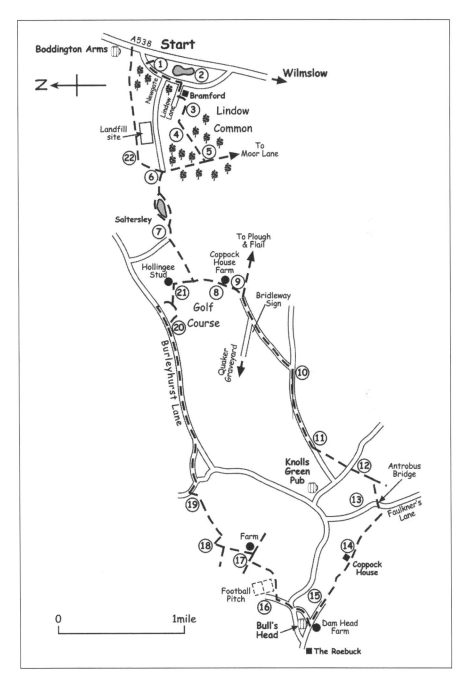

Wilmslow

183

Turn right (18), keeping the hedge on your right and cross a stile by a gate. The right of way goes round the edge of the field to the top-right corner and across a stile (or through the gate if open). Almost immediately, go over another stile and across a drainage ditch. Cross the next field, with its regular ridged pattern; bear slightly right, cross a footbridge and walk across a small field to the road (19). Turn right here (opposite to Holt House) and walk along Davenport Lane and then Burleyhurst Lane.

Turn left at the main road and, after 100m, turn right at the footpath sign (20) by the first gate on the right that you come to. Bear left across the golf course, keeping left of a hedge and trees. At a pond and waymark, turn left and walk between two rows of trees. At a gravel track, turn left and then right across a footbridge to join the drive to Hollingee.

Just before the farm, there is a stile on your right (21). Cross this and walk alongside the fence. After the fence turns to the left, continue in the same direction and cross the stile that is facing you. From here, turn left to head back to Saltersley Hall Farm. Since you have been here before, you should remember all of this, and it is virtually a straight line, but here are some points to note:

The next stile is sometimes tricky to find – it is tucked away in the top-left-hand corner of the field. Cross this, then turn right and continue in the same direction that you were walking – do not be tempted by the gap in the hedge. Just keep the hedge on your right and, at the stile on the farm drive, turn right to Saltersley Hall Farm.

This time, continue along the main farm track, taking you to the right of the lake. Keep going until you reach Newgate, but rather than continuing on the tarmac turn immediately left (6) along a wide track to pass a tennis court. After about 250m, turn right along the right of way just before a gate with a 'private' sign (22). Soon, pass to the right of a plantation and ignore a waymark pointing left. The route continues scross the landscaped Newgate landfill site – the noise you'll probably hear is due to the venting of methane gas from the decomposing rubbish. Where a wide track comes in from the left, you do a quick right and left and continue on the widening track, past the allotments ... to the A538 and then turn right to return to the car park. (Before doing so, note that you are temptingly close to the Boddington Arms.)

Walk: W6

Wilmslow and Knutsford:
a Bus 'n' Boots Walk

Starting Point: bus stop, Green Lane, Wilmslow

Map: OS Explorer 268 – Wilmslow, Macclesfield & Congleton

Length: 9½ miles (can be shortened by using intermediate bus stops)

Grade: Easy

Duration: 4 hours plus refreshment breaks

This walk uses the Connect 88 bus service from Wilmslow to Knutsford for the outward leg. Buses leave Green Lane at about 40 minutes past the hour. We of the bus-pass generation travel free most of the time – so long as we remember our pass! There's a timetable at the bus stop and online at http://tinyurl.com/33nn8mm. Note that the service does not operate on a Sunday and you must be sure to catch the Knutsford-bound Connect 88, not the one that goes to Altrincham at about the same time!

The walk returns across attractive (and mostly flat) countryside to Mobberley village, crosses the main Knutsford road and meanders across fields through part of Great Warford and back via Lindow to Wilmslow. When I last did this walk, I heard the hooting of a tawny owl and the hammering of a woodpecker, disturbed two buzzards, noticed a third being mobbed by crows, saw lots of lapwings and spotted a great crested grebe on Lindow Common lake. Not bad for one walk!

There are refreshment stops in abundance: four pubs and a café, so you really don't need to pack your sarnies. But always take a drink and waterproofs – and, of course, your camera.

The bus journey starts with a tour of Wilmslow, then goes all the way to the bus station in Knutsford, where there's a café inside the nearby Booth's supermarket. Turn right out of the bus station (1), cross the main road at the traffic lights and go almost straight ahead, towards the white tower of La Belle Epoque restaurant, down Church View and across King Street. Continue down Cotton Shop Yard to The Moor recreation area, then take a quick left and right to follow the Moor Pool on your left.

There may be better ways out of the town from this point, but this is

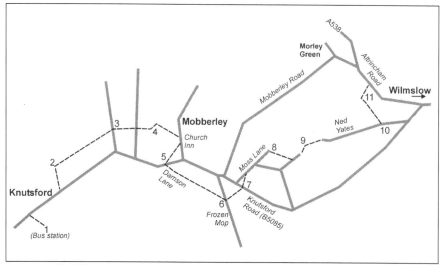

Simplified map of Knutsford to Wilmslow route: roads shown as grey lines

what I suggest: at the end of the iron railings between you and the pool, turn left along a wide track into a wood. After a few minutes, the trees thin out and you turn right on a narrower track between brambles. At a junction near a high steel gate, turn right into a housing estate. Go right at the next junction then left along the main road, walking away from Knutsford. After a few minute, turn left at the fire station into Parkgate Lane, cross the railway and head towards Parkgate Farm.

Just past the Royal Mail building on your right, turn right across a stile (2) and – bingo! – you are now in countryside. Cross the fields, following waymarks, stiles and electric fences. Pass a pool on your left, then skirt the edge of a wood to a stile in the far-left corner of the field. Cross this and continue slightly right to the bridge across Birkin Brook. Once over, fork left (waymark) and continue to Broadoak Lane. Cross this and take the footpath immediately opposite.

Walk along the right-hand edge of the field, passing several bird boxes –the big ones are for owls. Cross – **with extreme care** – the railway lines (3) then follow the path diagonally across the field towards Smithlane Farm, left of the Harmon factory (part of the old Ilford complex).

Cross Smith Lane and follow the footpath sign along a tarmac drive. Leave this by a stile on your left, then follow the raised track and cross a stream via a green-railed bridge. At a T-junction of paths, turn right,

St Wilfrid's and churchyard

following a fence on your right. At Valewood Farm (4), follow the waymarks that have you hopping left to right and back again (a very odd right of way!) then continue in the same direction as before.

Cross the next stile, turn left (waymark) then right after the next stile to head for Dairy Farm. Hit the road and continue to Mobberley church. It's worth having a wander around the churchyard, with graves that include that of Herbert Leigh Mallory, rector of St Wilfrid's from 1885 to 1904. The Everest explorer George Mallory (of the ill-fated 1924 Mallory and Irving expedition) was the son of Herbert and is said to have practised his abseiling skills on the church tower. The church is rarely open except for services, but it does have some interesting features, including the Mallory memorial window, that can be seen online at http://tinyurl.com/ctk28n. For a history of the village, go to www.mobberley.info.

Just across the road there's the Church Inn – tempting for a lunch stop. If you resist, four more pubs crop up in the next half hour, so you might as well give in now. From the church or pub, go downhill to pass the churchyard on your right, then through a kissing gate into Mobberley Field. Keep the cricket pitch and fence on your left, then cross a bridge and follow a well-trodden path to the main road. There's a bus stop on your right for the possibility of a lazy return to Wilmslow – but you've almost certainly just missed the bus, so let's carry on.

Cross the road (5) and walk along Mill Lane to pass the Bull's Head and then turn left, just before The Roebuck, into Damson Lane (which used to be Dam Lane, but Damson sounds more rural). This becomes an unsurfaced bridleway which, after a few minutes, bears right – but you continue straight ahead through a kissing gate. Go across the field, slightly right and cross a footbridge. Continue to the right of a hedge and towards the buildings of Coppock House Farm. Keep just right of the main building then follow the fence on your left. Two-thirds of the way along, change sides and continue to Faulkners Lane. The Frozen Mop is just a short way to your right, but you must have yielded to temptation by now, so turn left and cross Mobberley Brook via Antrobus Bridge (6).

Turn right at the footpath sign after the bridge and continue on a waymarked route, obeying any temporary diversions, to a very wet area that was submerged in several inches of water the last time I was there – see if you can find a drier way round the problem. Fork left from here to cross a stile, then head left to walk between a fence and trees, and through the end of a building (how bizarre!) to Knutsford Road.

Cross the main road (7) and follow the signpost into a field. A path leads from here across waymarked stiles to Moss Lane. Turn right onto this quiet lane and walk for about half a mile. Keep left at a junction, still along Moss Lane, until about 100m before a sign for Coppock House (same name, different house), where you reach a stile on your right (8). Cross this and follow the waymark to the next stile, then bear left and continue to yet another stile set in the fence on your left. Cross this and follow the path to a gateway, from where you bear right to the top corner of the field, then left along a bridleway around the Lindow Farm mobile home park (9). Keep left where the track meets a tarmac lane, and continue past the Ned Yates Garden Centre (or call in – there's a café).

At the next junction (10), turn left along Rotherwood Road and continue along a bridleway. About 200m after the last house, turn right along the 'restricted byway' and pass some dilapidated stables. Continue along Lindow Lane, cross Racecourse Road and enter Lindow Common (11). Pass the new 'mire area' – soon to be home for newts, dragonflies and reptiles – and, after a short distance, bear right to Black Lake (from the Welsh/Celtic "llyn ddu", corrupted to "Lindow"). Skim the far shore on a path that leads to Altrincham Road, the busy main road that leads into Wilmslow town centre, and you're almost home. Depending on where 'home'is!

THE CHESHIRE PEAKS CHALLENGE WALK

Starting point: Tegg's Nose Car Park SJ948733.

Length: 20 miles

Ascent: 900m/3000ft.

Duration: 9 hours – maybe more, maybe less!

I used this as a sponsored walk to raise money in 1995 for the David Lewis Centre for Epilepsy. You might like to do something similar, or do it just for fun. Some 14 years later, in 2009, I did just that with a group of friends (Rosie, Vron, Sue, John, Keith and Dave); we had an excellent day with good company and – thankfully – good weather. The total ascent is just four metres more than the height of Snowdon from sea level, and some of the views are, arguably, just as good. We completed the walk in less than 9 hours – the time it took way back in 1995, which just goes to show that regular walking helps to keep us fit!

Notes:

𝄞 Navigation is not difficult, but avoid a late start as this may mean returning in the dark through lonely countryside.

𝄞 20 miles is not to be underestimated, especially with over 3500ft of climbing. You'll need waterproof clothing, walking boots, supplies of food and at least 2 litres of liquid – more on a hot summer's day. There are no shops for supplies and the only refreshment points are the Cat and Fiddle (late coffee or early lunch) and The Poachers Inn in Bollington (but only open in the afternoon from Friday to Sunday).

𝄞 Timings refer to a 9.00am start, finishing by about 6.00pm if you walk briskly.

𝄞 Numbers in the description refer to the points on the sketch map.

The Route

1. **9.00am.** Walk south-east from Tegg's Nose car park (away from the road and the car park entrance) and down the steep "Sadler's Way"

From the starting point: looking towards Shutlingsloe

track, also marked by a stone sign for 'Langley and Forest Chapel'. Continue ahead along the tarmac lane at the bottom of the hill.

2. At Clough House Farm, keep left and follow the signs for Forest Chapel. Continue uphill, past a group of buildings (Lower Crooked Yard Farm).

3. Continue along the track for a few hundred metres and, 20m after a signpost on your right, turn left through a stile to follow a footpath passing diagonally across a field towards Hardingland Farm. Pass the farm on your left and follow the tarmac road uphill. In 50m or so, just as the road bears left, take a footpath to the right and enter the forest. Proceed to a junction of paths where you bear right and continue on the main track, signposted to Forest Chapel.

4. Pass a stone barn **(9.30am)**. Bear slightly left and go straight ahead through a stile (signposted Forest Chapel); the track goes steeply uphill through the forest and then down to Forest Chapel. On reaching the tarmac road at Forest Chapel, continue straight ahead on the tarmac road for a quarter of a mile to a T-junction and turn right. After another quarter of a mile, go over a crossroads and along a path signed to Shutlingsloe.

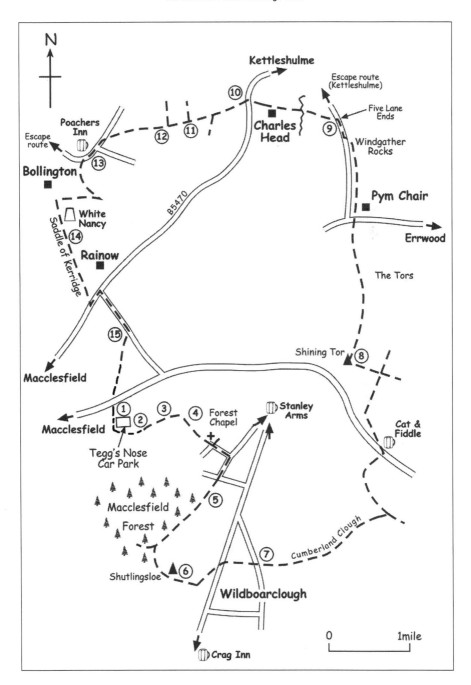

Margaret, Cathy & Diana – with a patriotic White Nancy for company – on the1995 walk

5. After a few minutes, fork left up some steps and follow the signed
    concessionary path, initially with forest on your right, to the top of
    Shutlingsloe. At 506m (1670ft) this is our first major peak (**10.35am**
    – 10-minute coffee break).

6. Continue over the top in roughly the same direction (east, follow
    arrow). Head downhill and turn right at a tarmac track. After a
    hundred metres or so, a sharp hairpin left takes you onto a rough
    track alongside woods on your right. Two gates and a stile lead to the
    road through Wildboarclough. Cross the bridge almost opposite,
    head towards a large farm (main building on left) and walk through
    the farmyard. Leave the farm by turning right on a tarmac lane, then
    cross the road to a gated track leading to Cumberland Clough.

7. Once in the clough, cross the footbridge and walk uphill with the
    stream on your right. Keep to the path nearest to the stream – do not
    take any side-turnings. At the waterfall at the top of the clough, turn
    left ('Cat & Fiddle' sign). Climb steeply uphill to a Public Footpath
    sign at a T-junction where you turn left again and walk across open
    moorland, towards the Cat & Fiddle (**12.00 noon** – 515m, 1690 feet).
    Cross the busy road and turn left yet again. Go downhill and turn
    right at a Public Footpath sign. Continue on a track, ignoring the left

fork to the Peak View café. Pass an 'Errwood' footpath sign and then, after a further 200m, turn left at the sign to Shining Tor.

8. Climb to Shining Tor **(12.30pm)**, the highest point in Cheshire – 559m, 1845ft; you can visit the trig point by way of a concessionary stile. Continue northwards along the entire ridge-plateau of the Tors until you reach a 'Windgather' signpost. Fork right here and follow the signed concessionary path.

    Just before the huge gritstone crags, pause for a 20-minute lunch break **(1.30pm)**. Suitably refreshed, walk for a short distance and fork left to join the road by way of the climbers' access path below the rocks. Turn right at the road and walk downhill to a crossroads ('Fivelane Ends' on the OS map). Turn left here then, very soon, go right at a gateway with a footpath sign to Charles Head.

9. Walk downhill, with the wall on your right. The path soon begins to climb, passing through two wide wall gaps, then heads downhill and over a stile towards a house and outbuilding. At the bottom of the hill, turn left along a track and – just past the house on the right – go through a gate and turn immediately right. Continue downhill to the right of an overgrown hedge and cross a footbridge.

    Climb the facing steep hill towards Charles Head – head left to a barn then go further uphill and along an old track sloping up to the right. Walk along a short length of cobbles towards the buildings of Charles Head and uphill to the highest point, overlooking Kettleshulme **(2.15pm** – about 350m, 1155ft). Follow the main track to the road.

10. Cross the busy road to a wide farm track. After a short distance, cross a stile on the left and alongside a cattle grid. The path enters a small plantation of young trees but soon becomes sunken and overgrown so, where necessary, keep to the higher ground to the right. After half a mile, marked by a fence ahead, cross the stream and go over a stile. After about 200m, reach an intersection of three paths where, in June 2009, waymarks had been removed. Turn right, downhill, along a sunken track with a wall on your right.

11. Cross a stile just before Further Harrop farm, and walk past the farm. Continue straight ahead and down another sunken track to a T-junction marked with a group of trees. Turn left along the tree-lined track. Head left, go through a gateway, then bear right across a footbridge.

12. Where the track meets Harrop Brook, turn left (do not cross the bridge) and pass a house, staying on a tarmac track. This leads past various other houses, but keep your eyes peeled so that you turn left at Cheshire Hunt Cottages – on the site of the eponymous pub. Cross a field and bear right to a stile leading to a road **(3.30pm)** where you turn left towards Bollington.

13. Immediately before The Poachers Inn, turn left along a track. At the end of the track, turn left along a road and walk past the industrial buildings. Ignore the first signpost on the right and then, after a couple of hundred metres, turn right (Gritstone Trail sign) uphill. At the top of the hill, turn left and stagger up the stepped track to White Nancy **(4.15pm)** – 310m, 1023ft.

14. From the White Nancy monument, follow the path along the entire length of the ridge (almost due south) – do not take any side-paths leading off the ridge. Towards the very end of the ridge, after a trig point, bear left to the main road. Turn left here and then take the first turn on your right.

Walk up here for just a short distance and turn left through a gate alongside the 'Road Narrows' and 'Penny Lane' signs. Walk up the grassy slope and, at the top, turn right through the gate (if open) or over the ladder stile about 50yds to the right. Follow the wall on your right and cross a stile alongside a clump of trees; turn right and almost immediately cross another stile to follow the Gritstone Trail marker and walk alongside a wall (*not* the track bearing to the left). Walk across the middle of the next field and pass through a kissing gate. Go downhill to a bridge and turn left (uphill); cross a stile and head for yet another stile leading to the busy main road. Cross this (with care), turn left uphill and, very soon, go through the gate on your right.

15. Continue through the field along a well-used and waymarked path (with stiles), almost in a straight line to the road. Turn right at the road and then left into the car park at Tegg's Nose **(5.45pm)** – 350m, 1155ft.

Congratulations – you've made it!

Also from Sigma Leisure:

All-Terrain Pushchair Walks
Cheshire
Norman Buckley

30 graded walks, from level routes around pretty Cheshire villages to more adventurous hikes across the hillsides. Detailed directions and a map are provided for each route, together with some stunning photographs.

£7.95

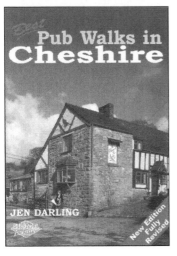

Best Pub Walks in Cheshire
2nd Edition
Jen Darling

This is the second edition of a guidebook to the walks and pubs of Cheshire.

"I was delighted to be asked to put a few words on paper … this book brings together a series of suggestions for your enjoyment."
– John Ellis, Cheshire Tourism

£8.99

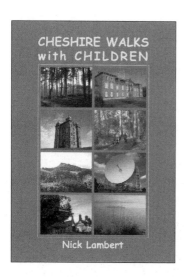

Cheshire Walks With Children 2nd Edition
Nick Lambert

Now completely revised and updated, this was the first in our "walks with children" series and has quickly become a firm favourite. There are 30 walks, ranging in length, together with things to look out for and questions to answer along the way make it an entertaining book for young and old alike.

£8.99

50 Best Cycle Rides in Cheshire
Edited by Graham Beech

"Every cyclist should be leaping into their saddles with this new book."
– The Cheshire Magazine.
Completely updated
£8.95

Wirral Walks 2nd Edition
100 miles of the best walks in the area
Anthony Annakin-Smith

A completely revised and updated edition of this popular collection of 25 walks from around 2 to 10 miles, covering a total of 100 miles through the best of the local landscape. The author's careful research highlights the interesting and unusual features seen along each route.

£8.99

Discovering Manchester
2nd Edition
Barry Worthington

This stylish walking guide doubles as a detailed account of the city's architecture, its history and tourism attractions. There are walks throughout Manchester including such major entertainment and cultural centres as the Bridgewater Hall, Urbis, the Museum of Science and Industry, the Lowry and many more. Explore the entire city – from the Corn Exchange to G-Mex, from the Cathedral to Affleck's Palace.

£10.99

Available May 2010

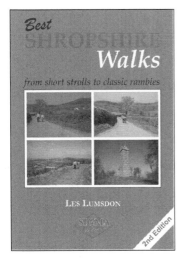

Best Shropshire Walks
2nd Edition
From short strolls to classic rambles
Les Lumsdon

A new revised edition of this much loved guide contains 36 walks, including 12 completely new routes, located in all parts of the county. Several walks feature fine hill walking on the Welsh borders and others start from delightful villages and hamlets in the north and east of the county.

£8.99

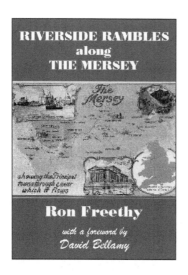

Riverside Rambles along The Mersey
Ron Freethy
with a foreword by David Bellamy

This is far more than a guidebook for walkers, it is also a portrait of one of the world's greatest rivers – once so polluted that Michael Heseltine described the state of the Mersey basin as "an affront to civilised society". Nowadays, however, salmon pass through the estuary, wildlife abounds along the entire catchment area and a rich and diverse coastline attracts a huge variety of birdlife.

Featuring 30 walks short, gentle walks (mostly circular). Explore the unique scenery, ecology and heritage of this area.
£8.99

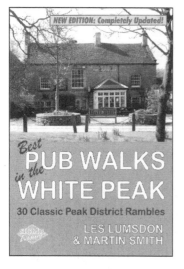

Best Pub Walks in the Dark Peak &
Best Pub Walks in the White Peak
Les Lumsdon and Martin Smith

These two books, both by Les Lumsdon and Martin Smith, provide comprehensive coverage of the entire Peak District. Inspiring walks and welcoming pubs enable walkers to appreciate the history, landscape and personalities of the area. These books were published by us originally in the 1980s and have recently been completely updated to ensure accuracy. Each book costs
£8.99

Archaeology Walks in The Peak District
Ali Cooper

These walks explore archaeological sites where there are visible pre-historic features in the landscape: Bronze age barrows, stone circles, caves, mines and much more. Walks are from 3 to 12 miles and are fully illustrated. The book includes an introduction to the study of archaeology and a glossary of the terminology used. Brief descriptions of the major finds on the walks are included, plus a bibliography for those who wish to delve deeper. Ali Cooper has an MA in archaeology and is a keen outdoors enthusiast.

£8.99

Peak District Walking – On The Level
Norman Buckley

Some folk prefer easy walks, and sometimes there's just not time for an all-day yomp. In either case, this is definitely a book to keep on your bookshelf. Norman Buckley has had considerable success with "On The Level" books for the Lake District and the Yorkshire Dales.

The walks are ideal for family outings and the precise instructions ensure that there's little chance of losing your way. Well-produced maps encourage everybody to try out the walks - all of which are well scattered across the Peak District.

£7.95

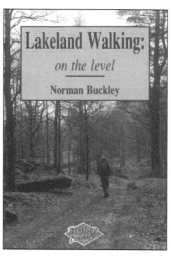